FETISHIZED

FETISHIZED

A Reckoning with
Yellow Fever, Feminism,
and Beauty

KAILA YU

 CROWN
NEW YORK

CROWN
An imprint of the Crown Publishing Group
A division of Penguin Random House LLC
1745 Broadway
New York, NY 10019
crownpublishing.com
penguinrandomhouse.com

Lyrics from "Candy Coated Sugar Sex" by Kaila Yu on pages 162 and 163 are used by permission of Embryo Productions.
Art on pages ii–iii from Shutterstock.com/Here.

Library of Congress Cataloging-in-Publication Data
Names: Yu, Kaila, 1979– author
Title: Fetishized : a reckoning with yellow fever, feminism, and beauty / Kaila Yu.
Description: New York : Crown Publishing, 2025.
Identifiers: LCCN 2025000701 (print) | LCCN 2025000702 (ebook) |
ISBN 9780593728017 hardcover | ISBN 9780593728024 ebook
Subjects: LCSH: Yu, Kaila, 1979– | Women singers—United States—Biography |
Women rock musicians—United States—Biography | Models (Persons)—United States—
Biography | Asian American women—Biography | Asian American women—Public
opinion | Asian American women—Sexual behavior | Nylon Pink (Musical group) |
Orientalism—United States—History—21st century | LCGFT: Autobiographies
Classification: LCC ML420.Y77 A3 2025 (print) | LCC ML420.Y77 (ebook) |
DDC 782.42166092 [B]—dc23/eng/20250529
LC record available at https://lccn.loc.gov/2025000701
LC ebook record available at https://lccn.loc.gov/2025000702

Hardcover ISBN 978-0-593-72801-7
Ebook ISBN 978-0-593-72802-4

Editor: Amy Li
Production editor: Joyce Wong
Text designer: Amani Shakrah
Production: Heather Williamson
Copy editor: Nancy Tan
Proofreaders: Sigi Nacson, Katy Miller
Publicist: Lauren Chung
Marketer: Kimberly Lew

Manufactured in the United States of America

1 2 3 4 5 6 7 8 9

First Edition

The authorized representative in the EU for product safety and compliance is Penguin Random House Ireland, Morrison Chambers, 32 Nassau Street, Dublin D02 YH68, Ireland, https://eu-contact.penguin.ie.

To Kitty, the most beautiful and loyal being I've ever known

Asiaphile (noun): The term applies to a non-Asian person particularly a white man who has yellow fever. Thinks all Asian chicks are hot, usually can't tell the difference between a homely and a cute one just as long as she is Asian.

Lucy Liu is Asiaphile's favorite.

—Urban Dictionary

Fetish (noun): an object of irrational reverence or obsessive devotion

—*Merriam-Webster's Collegiate Dictionary,*
Eleventh Edition

CONTENTS

CONTENTS

AUTHOR'S NOTE

This is a work of nonfiction based on my memories, interviews, journals, and conversations. To protect the privacy of certain individuals, most names and identifying details have been changed. While my point of view has been colored by trauma and the resulting dissociation and emotional flattening, I have recounted the incidences and experiences in these essays as faithfully and truthfully as I remember them.

INTRODUCTION

An absurdly wealthy white male friend with a famous predilection for Asian women once told me, "I prefer Asian women, because if you line up a row of a hundred Asian women and a row of a hundred white women, the Asian group will be way more attractive than the white group."

I rolled my eyes, thinking, *Not true; it's just that you, an Asiaphile, think practically all Asian women are beautiful.* But I smiled and said nothing.

Even more recently, I wandered into a store on Melrose with a date. "You should wear this," he said with a laugh, jokingly pointing to a dominatrix-style leather corseted bodysuit like something Lady Gaga would wear onstage. As we passed the register, I stopped to play with two handsome huskies, one pure white and one with an unusual dappled brown coat and cornflower-blue eyes.

"You know, this one can say 'Ruff, I love you,'" said the dogs' owner—a portly man in his sixties with wild, curly brown hair—as if to impress us. "Let me show you."

He waved his hands in the air. Both dogs proceeded to howl, but not quite as he described.

"Where are you guys from?" he asked, seeming eager to chat. "I'm that rare LA native," he added, referring to the fact that so many in Hollywood are hopeful transplants, chasing a silvery dream of fame or riches.

"Oh, me, too," I said. I grew up in Southern California, although more accurately, in the muggy Inland Empire.

"No, where are you *from* from," he insisted.

I knew what he was asking and yet answered accordingly, not needing to make this a teachable moment. "My parents are from Taiwan."

I held my breath in anticipation of what would drop out of his mouth next. My date hadn't been familiar with the concept of the Asian fetish, and now he was observing it in the wild.

"Asian girls are the most beautiful women," said the dog owner, gazing at me as if I were a glazed doughnut. Curious about what he would say next, I let him continue. "I want to start a class where Asian women teach Jewish women how to be the best wives. They could learn a thing or two. You ever heard of Gloria Steinem? Yeah, women's liberation is the worst thing that ever happened to American women."

Note that Asiaphiles often espouse that Asian women make the best wives, something you rarely hear out of the mouths of Asian men. The craziest thing about the Asian fetish is how confidently men announce it, with absolutely no shame and a good measure of pride.

When I was growing up in the '80s and '90s, Asiaphiles were limited to creepy, pasty fifty-year-old men like the dog owner at the clothing store. Nowadays, with the popularity of K-pop and anime, and the increased visibility of Asian women in social media, TV, and film, it seems the Asian fetish has been accepted as mainstream. Handsome, tall hipsters with tattoos and famous musicians proudly proclaim their love for Asian women. It's like everyone simply accepted that white men love Asian women, reminding me of the blog *Stuff White People Like*, which went viral in 2008, listing Asian girls as number eleven. Although the blog was meant to be satirical, it states, "95% of white males have at one point in their lives experienced yellow fever." Yellow fever doubles as the name of an unwanted disease transmitted by mosquitoes, further derogating the term. Like mosquitoes, fetishists suck the humanity out of Asian women, turning them into 2D sex objects. The "Asian Girls" entry has more than twenty-three thousand impassioned comments, whereas other blog posts average around a thousand comments. That blog post has become only more relevant today.

Today, Asiaphiles are everywhere I turn. Open up TikTok, turn on the radio, and I'm met with musicians flaunting their unfiltered appreciation for Asian women as if they were commodities rather than breathing women. Multiplatinum artist The Weeknd has been accused of having an Asian fetish, rapping, "Got a sweet Asian chick, she go lo mein," reducing us to bodies and menu items. Asian women populate his music videos as sexually submissive props, while he's been criticized for featuring few

Black women. His effortless falsetto and slick beats belie a toxic masculinity and misogyny that fuse desire with dominance. The explicit version of his "Pretty" music video features graphic scenes of a naked Asian woman playing his girlfriend. When she cheats on him with another Black man, he shoots her during coitus in vicious revenge. This heinous scene is a brutal reminder that Asian women, no matter how desired and fetishized, are disposable.

The actor Donald Glover, aka the rapper Childish Gambino, is another artist accused of yellow fever. There's a graph online titled "Analysis of Childish Gambino's Use of Asians in His Lyrics," analyzing each of his albums and how many times Asians are mentioned. *Camp* takes the lead with thirty-plus mentions. In that album, he directly addressed the accusation in his song "Kids (Keep Up)":

But they say I got a fetish, nah, I'm skippin' all of it

He goes on to explain that different rules and politics come into place when dating Black or white girls. Translation: "White and Black girls are too complicated, too vocal, too opinionated"— statements Asiaphiles love to dish out. "Asian girls are sweeter, easier," they say, but what they really mean is that they believe Asian women are docile and easy to mold to male desires. It's a myth, a convenient fantasy, that removes our complexity and individuality and is used to pit us against other women. However, in an interview with HardKnock.tv, Glover explained that it's just easier to be with Asian women because it's simpler politically. When he dates Asians, no one blinks twice, whereas he faces judgment if he dates a white or Black woman.

True or not, on another track, the incredibly catchy "You See

Me," Glover further confirms his Asian favoritism by rapping in the chorus repeatedly, "Asian girls everywhere, UCLA." Watching Glover's magnetic live performance of the song at Brandeis University on YouTube, it's hard not to feel flattered as he shouts this line. The crowd chants alongside him, roaring and throwing hands in the air as the lyrics are projected behind Glover. My knee-jerk response is "Yes! Asian girls are the best!" as if vindicated for the years growing up hungering for acceptance while invisible and undesired. But beneath that initial validation, I know the unfortunate truth: We're not celebrated for our strength, humanity, and intelligence. We're reduced to a fantasy fitting a male-dominance narrative.

The lyrics in the main verse of the song degrade us even further. Glover says that he doesn't mind cumming on a girl's face if he doesn't love her, and affirms his preference for Asian women, rapping:

Forget these white girls
I need some variation

There's even a line neatly tying together the Asian model minority myth and the hypersexualized submissive Asian trope, calling out Asian women overachievers who succeed, or "suck seed" (referencing a blow job).

Glover's lyrics illustrate a curious trait seemingly unique to Asiaphiles, denigrating other races of women to prop up their Asian preference. His words suggest that white women are the standard and Asian women are the "variation," othering Asian women in his fetishization, as fetishists have done throughout history. Overall, this nonsensical song is a strange ode to Asian women that simultaneously glorifies and objectifies them. He even randomly drops in half-Asian actress Olivia Munn's name, stating he hopes he can hook up with her.

At face value, these mentions could be compliments. Growing up, Asians were so invisible, objectification was better than nothing. It felt like we were elevated onto pedestals—hypersexualized, yes, but at least visible. *Famous musicians think we're hot!* As a nineties kid listening to Guns N' Roses and Skid Row, I couldn't have imagined that my favorite rock stars—Sebastian Bach, Trent Reznor, Rivers Cuomo, and Perry Farrell—would have Asian wives.

Yellow fever seemed harmless enough. Couldn't one argue these men just had a preference?

It's a bit more complicated than that. I don't believe that most men who date Asian women have a fetish. I'm also not accusing anyone of an Asian fetish if they fall in love with an Asian woman and also value her individuality, independence, and autonomy. Men often ask me what the difference is between a fetish and a preference. It's difficult to answer; it's truly a case-by-case basis, and the line between the two can be quite blurry. I want to stress again that not all white men who date an Asian woman have a fetish! But some important things to consider include: Does he value the Asian woman in question for her unique mind, thoughts, and passions, or is it purely about aesthetics, the mere fact that she's Asian, or stereotypical personality traits? How much sexualization and objectification is at play? Is she someone who just happens to be Asian, or is he interested in her only because she's Asian? Are Asian women interchangeable sex objects in his mind?

The Asian fetish is more than mere preference and admiration of physical features like hair, skin, and eyes. It's a myopic, generalized belief that Asian women inherently embody traits of submissiveness and obedience. Because of these imagined ideals, Asiaphiles date Asian women exclusively, actively seeking them out and openly declaring them superior to other races, especially sexually. They may only watch Asian pornography. These men consider Asian women to be interchangeable, like collectible souvenirs. They care little about individual nuances and personality. It's not rare for them to say our anatomy is physiologically different, like we're another species of women or kinky, forbidden aliens with unique sexual superpowers.

Asiaphiles are the type of guy in a perfectly happy relationship with an Asian woman who still follows dozens of scantily clad Asian Instagram models, often slipping into their DMs. They're the Asiaphile boyfriend or husband of your Asian girlfriend who whispers to you, "You're so sexy," when her back is turned. After my girlfriend broke up with one of these men, he texted her, "It's no big deal. There are hundreds of even more stunning Asian women in Los Angeles." In 2021, an old white man went viral for a now-deleted TikTok, advising other white men hoping to date Asian women. His advice was to head to Asia if "interested in dating or marrying beautiful Asian girls . . . out of your league." He said the Asian girl will inevitably leave you in four to five years, but you can just trade her in for a new one. Similarly, my wealthy white friend is still single fifteen years later. He's over fifty years old, yet still dating young Asian women. He's aged, but his Asian girlfriends haven't. They're exchangeable as long as they remain below thirty years old.

Over the course of my career as a pinup model, I've met hundreds of men like him. Many were fans of my idol, Sung-Hi Lee, and other Asian pinups before me. I'm certain all moved on to some other little ingenue once I quit modeling and aged out. We weren't lifted onto pedestals at all; we were consumed and erased.

On the flip side, when I call out Asian fetishism on social media, I'm swiftly accused of having a white fetish. The accusation is absurd since I've dated men of different ethnicities, including Asian. Also, fetishism doesn't operate in the opposite direction. The Asian fetish is rooted in colonialism, with Asian women raped, sold, and captured as spoils of wars. Asian women, conversely, have no history of conquering and colonizing white nations and raping white men.

What does exist is internalized racism—a powerful force shaping some of the dating preferences of Asian women, including my own. The weight of the Asian fetish, media representations, and the underlying self-hate of internalized racism drove my career choices as a teenager and young adult. My successes felt like winning, but they were simply another form of erasure. In the early 2000s, Asian women had little to no representation in mainstream media. I found validation in living up to the sexualized Asian women I saw on film and TV and pursued a career as a pinup model in my early twenties. This same lack of representation also emasculated Asian men as sexless nerds, while glorifying white men as the pinnacle of masculinity, leading Asian women to gravitate toward white men as the ultimate ideal.

My error wasn't just in participating in these tropes. It was taking them to their extreme and making them my entire life's goal, my focus, my career. I believed it was either that or disappear entirely, becoming invisible and, in my mind, eminently unlovable.

Because of these media influences, I felt the straightest path to empowerment was through courting the white male gaze. The Asian fetish existed decades before me, but I willingly perpetuated it. As much as I was a victim of society's influences, I was also complicit, choosing to become a pinup model and basking in the attention. I altered my body to fit Western beauty standards, posed nude for the camera, and played into tropes. I had agency in performing yellow fever fantasies, at least to some extent.

———

I sometimes wonder why my life took such an unexpected turn. How did I end up like this?

My parents, still married, are hardworking immigrants who provided everything I needed. I was well educated with a degree from UCLA. I should have gotten a respectable job with a 401(k). Perhaps I was just a product of the early aughts. My notoriety came during a post-feminism era when many women were shedding their clothing and inhibitions. *Maxim, FHM,* and other lad magazines were at the height of popularity, the porn star Jenna Jameson was a mainstream celebrity, and Paris Hilton had catapulted to heights of fame through a leaked sex tape.

Even after leaving modeling to pursue a singing career, I inadvertently found myself continuing to fall into hypersexualized Asian tropes. At first I crafted a more innocent and wholesome persona for music, but it was so much easier to perform the sexual vixen. As my solo career began to take off via my eroticized image, and later when my band Nylon Pink toured the world in skintight vinyl dresses, I reasoned that though I capitalized on nubile desirability to attract listeners, at least I wasn't removing my clothing. Still, despite the attention and the warm beam of the male gaze, I felt empty, spiraling into the depths of drug addiction.

It was only after getting sober that I faced my choices head-on and considered their implications. Before sobriety I lived an unexamined life, never believing I would reach forty—in fact hoping I didn't. Accordingly, I lived in the moment and never made plans, chasing glimmerings of whims and fancies. After shining a light on my past, I'm conflicted. I'm proud of the magazine covers and spreads I shot in my early twenties. However, I also doubt I would have posed nude if more Asian American female role models were available in the media when I was growing up. As Margaret Cho said in her 2002 *Notorious C.H.O.* show, Asians in our era had limited dreams. "Maybe someday . . . I could be an extra on *M*A*S*H*," said Cho. "Maybe someday . . . I could play Arnold's girlfriend on *Happy Days*. Maybe someday . . . I could play a hooker in something."

———

Today things are improving for Asian women worldwide, but as we saw with the Atlanta spa shootings in March 2021, we're still violently objectified, resulting in horrific consequences. I can't help but feel I played a part in perpetrating and mainstreaming yellow fever during my pinup modeling and singing careers. I don't believe I was a healthy influence for the thousands of young Asian women who reached out, telling me it was their dream to become an import model. Although the Asian fetish existed long before import models, we took the already sexualized image of the "meek" and "reserved" Asian woman and repackaged her into an Americanized pinup bombshell with blond highlights and breast implants, creating an even wider audience for the Asian fetish.

This essay collection explores my choices and exploits within the framework of society, yellow fever, and the lies I told myself to get by. It examines the formative experiences shaping my modeling and singing careers, before ultimately transforming into a version of enlightenment. I'm still chiseling away at the layers between the pleasurable applause of the chauvinistic gaze and my feminist ideals, especially at an age when my physical attractiveness is quickly waning. I know I'll be unraveling these unconscious beliefs—woven by media and culture like a silent, constantly spinning spider—for a lifetime. Luckily, once exposed to light, these cobwebbed ideas and programming can be swiped away. I hope this proves a cautionary tale so others might avoid some of my more painful choices.

DADDY

As a child, I wanted to be like Ariel in *The Little Mermaid*. The iconic Disney film was my favorite growing up. I gravitated toward it because of an inherent love for the ocean, charmed by Sebastian the Crab's "Under the Sea" performance, surrounded by clapping scallops and colorful twirling fish. I found a kindred spirit in the stunning, fiery-haired mermaid's rebellious nature, wishing for a more significant and fulfilling life outside her strict home. But beneath its bubbly surface and happy ending, the story whispered that a woman's most significant power came from being desired by men.

While the Disney version is frothy and colorful with a perfectly neat happy ending, the original Hans Christian Andersen fairy tale, written in Denmark in 1837, is practically a horror movie. Not only does the mermaid lose the prince and commit suicide, but she also endures excruciating pain and risks safety and health to transform her body for a man. In the Andersen narrative, when her tail transforms into legs, the pain is so unbearable she passes out, and she's cursed with the feeling of sharp knives with every step, feet bleeding from these wounds. She also allows the sea witch Ursula to violently cut off her tongue. This contrasts sharply with the Disney film, where Ursula (inspired by the famed drag queen Divine) captures her voice in a conch shell instead.

At the heart of both tales—Disney's sanitized version and Andersen's gothic horror—lies the same truth: to be loved by a man, you must diminish yourself. This message is especially evident in the Disney film. Prince Eric falls in love with Ariel without knowing her name or having a spoken conversation with her. As she's mute, he monologues at her while she lustfully bats her eyelashes in outright admiration. Ursula reinforces this idea, singing in "Poor Unfortunate Souls" that women don't need voices to catch a man; instead, makeup, accessories, and body language are superior. Opinions and personality are irrelevant, even annoying, according to her.

I ate up and internalized the misogyny of the film's messaging, dreaming princess fantasies of being rescued by a savior prince. The love and adoration of a man was the goal. To get it, all I needed to do was morph myself into his dream girl, erase myself, and gaze up at him with dewy doe eyes. I didn't realize I was absorbing an anti-feminist blueprint and becoming a mere girl-shaped thing waiting for male validation. I craved recognition and affection but received none. It left me with a phantom limb of a heart, voraciously hungry for male adoration with a ravenousness that could never be satiated.

In the movie, Ariel's relationship with her father, King Triton, cut through me like a blade. He worships his daughter, cherishing her beauty and talent, even when trying to control her. Despite being a strict disciplinarian, all his actions are threaded with love. My father was much more like King Triton from Andersen's original story.

In Andersen's tale, the Sea King is emotionally unavailable, silent, and detached, never interacting with the little mermaid, much like my own father. In response, she grasps for validation from the prince, a complete stranger. She settles for scraps and crumbs as he treats her like a cherished pet rather than a respected partner. The prince allows her to sleep on a velvet cushion by his door, and when he marries another woman, the little mermaid marches behind, holding the bride's train. Her lack of self-worth likely stemmed from the absence of her father's affection.

For me, what my young self interpreted as a lack of affectionate fatherly love was a deafening silence. My father was a good and solid man who worked tirelessly to provide food, shelter, and structure—just like the Sea King in Andersen's tale—but I could never find his eyes on me. Once, while still in elementary school, he gave my brother a rare hug in the living room. Eager to join in, I sprang forward to embrace him, but my dad stopped me, saying firmly, "No, that wouldn't be appropriate," in Chinese. I don't remember ever seeing him hug my brother again. But it spoke volumes to my young self that he would hug my brother but not me.

Embarrassed and humiliated, I never asked for affection again. What hurt most was that he could be captivated—just not by me. I envied his obsessive dedication to his manicured vegetable garden. Instead of playing with me, his hands tenderly pruned his tomato plants, eyes softening as he gently plucked out chubby, giant, four-inch-long tomato hornworms, bright green and blending into the plant stems. I would sometimes help him locate these sneaky caterpillars, and I didn't realize at the time that he was trying to share his world with me. On weekends, my father would also take my brother and me and our cousins to the beach or on other excursions. Although he didn't speak much, he was always physically available, present at family gatherings, and trying to tend to our needs in his own way. He had no idea I needed oceans of verbal validation and affection.

Like me, my father was an introvert, but his silence suffocated me, a black hole drowning all my achievements. There's a popular meme circulated in Asian American circles called High Expectations Asian Dad. The father in the meme is stern, unloving, and always disappointed. My father was the embodiment of this meme, though without the expectations. He wasn't disappointed in me—he didn't appear to care enough to be. As an adult, I now understand he did the best he could, growing up in his own emotionally devoid household. But I'd be lying if I said the complete absence of his praise didn't carve a deep chasm of self-doubt. Though I've always considered him honorable, trustworthy, and perennially present in the practical sense, there was no intimate relationship between my father and me despite our similar personalities. I hardly remember speaking to him growing up. *It's not his fault*, I told myself. *Many Asian fathers are like this.* His silence spoke louder than harsh words ever did, and I often questioned if I was worthy of existing.

One summer in junior high, I tried to impress my dad with an end-of-summer performance. I gathered my cousins, and we performed scenes from *The Little Mermaid* and the Alvin and the

Chipmunks version of "Cinderella" and danced to Janet Jackson's "Escapade." All summer, we practiced, and I brimmed with anticipation as we gnawed on my father's sticky, sweet, barbecued ribs and spit out watermelon seeds in our backyard. I was convinced this was the moment, finally, that my dad would beam with pride, and I would no longer be the daughter who floated through the house like air.

But during showtime, as we sang, "Es-ca-pade. We'll have a good time," along with Janet Jackson, throwing our hands in the air and twirling in mimicry of her music video choreography, I noticed my dad was no longer in the audience; he'd left midway through and never returned. He never mentioned the performance afterward, as if it had never happened, as if I was so inconsequential, so easily erased, that the memory of me vanished from his mind the moment he stood up. Unlike Disney's King Triton, who was so upset that Ariel skipped out on her solo that he canceled the concert altogether, my father didn't seem to notice my existence. Or at least that's how it felt. I never performed for him again.

My father provided stability and privilege, sacrificing his own dreams for our family. This was his way of showing love, but I longed for the demonstrative love and emotional support that never came. That little girl wanted her father to smile with pride after the performance designed to impress him. She needed a hug, some small gesture of affirmation that her daddy loved her. But that physical and verbal type of love never showed up. As a result,

I've always felt emotionally alone, not deserving of the love and adoration others received effortlessly.

I strived for perfection, believing that if I got straight A's, mastered Chopin's nocturnes, danced Taiwanese aboriginal dances with bells on my ankles—then maybe he would see me. Yet my father remained hidden behind the black-and-white paper walls of the *Los Angeles Times*. No matter how diligently I performed, his gaze remained fixed on stories of other people's lives. Was it because I wasn't pretty enough? I felt he wouldn't even notice if I disappeared. My accomplishments were like ghosts, haunting the spaces between us. I could be perfect but never real. I didn't realize then that his silence wasn't apathy; he sacrificed his own dreams so we were never lacking.

Even before I fell in love with *The Little Mermaid*, I wanted to be like the rabbit in the children's book *The Velveteen Rabbit*, transformed from a stuffed toy into something tangible, not through achievement but through love. In the tale, the rabbit is adored until his whiskers fall off, his pink lining turns gray, and he loses shape—but love keeps him perfect. I envied that kind of fondness that saw through imperfection. But I kept performing—perfect grades, perfect piano pieces, perfect silence—waiting for my dad to acknowledge me.

Where was my proof that love could make me whole? Well, Andersen's little mermaid isn't loved and cherished by the men in her life and dies tragically. In contrast, Ariel from *The Little Mermaid* is adored by both her father and Prince Eric because of her loveliness, and she lives happily ever after, buoyed by love she didn't need to earn.

I was no fairy-tale princess—plain and dismissed by boys at school and overlooked by my father. Ariel barely had to lift a finger to be loved, while I didn't get an ounce of attention despite pushing myself to excel at everything I did. As I navigated this humbling invisibility, as a little girl, I believed that love, or at least attention, was only bestowed on the beautiful. If I couldn't dazzle, I would remain insignificant and continue to slip through life unnoticed.

I spent the next decades of my life chasing beauty.

GEISHA

When Arthur Golden's book *Memoirs of a Geisha* was published, it became a cultural phenomenon for supposedly amplifying Asian stories, but together with the later hit movie, it instead helped shape America's idea of Asian women and buttressed yellow fever. The book was evocative and gorgeously written, but the essential thrust is a simple tale of patriarchal yore: the younger, more beautiful woman always wins. It told a story about Asian women but portrayed us in a specific light, one rooted in stereotypes, romantic Orientalism, and an antiquated Asia.

I devoured the book, desperate for stories of women who looked like me, entranced by the Cinderella storyline, not realizing until much later that the plot was little more than a misogynistic fairy tale centered around the exotic fantasies of white men. In this piece of pure fiction, Sayuri, the "Asian Cinderella," is a sex worker with no hope of ever becoming a princess. Instead, she's required to sell her virginity to the highest bidder. The best she can dream for is to become the mistress of a married man, allowing him to become her sugar daddy.

In the opening pages, Golden tells us Sayuri was sold into slavery at nine years old and groomed to be an underage plaything for men. After the film debuted, the famed movie critic Robert Ebert opined that Western audiences weren't interested in gritty, accurate portrayals of Asian female subjugation and sexual slavery. They wanted to see Asian women in a dance of desire and strategy combined with exoticism and sex. He added that if the film were about white women, Western viewers would clearly view it as a child prostitution movie.

Sayuri's character is also highly underdeveloped. She has an idiotic childlike obsession, devotion, and love for a man known as the Chairman. She first meets him at the age of nine, when he is forty-five. It's framed as a love story, but he's the ultimate groomer playing the long game. In Sayuri's voice as a little girl, Golden writes, "He was looking at me as a musician might look at his instrument just before he begins to play, with understanding and mastery. . . . How I would have loved to be the instrument he played!" After that first meeting, the Chairman secretly orchestrates the path allowing Sayuri to become the most famous geisha in Kyoto.

Sayuri's rivalry with the jealous elder reigning geisha, Hatsumomo, captivated me—the two women striving to be the most renowned in a bubble of women dedicating their entire existence to serving men. Hatsumomo was the Wicked Queen to Sayuri's Snow White. Her beauty afforded fame and accomplishments, such as earning back her geisha purchase price by the time she was twenty, an unusual feat. She first appears in the movie forming out of the shadows, like a ghost before a Japanese shoji screen, dressed in a black silk kimono lined with gold embroidery. More stunning than a doll, her bloodred lips pop boldly from her spectral white face. Her face is elegantly melancholy as a servant sparks a flint behind her for good luck. Her exquisiteness masks her true character, filled with sociopathic jealousy, misery, and mistreatment of everyone around her. She's more venomous spider than swan. Hatsumomo's name translates into "first peach"—fitting, as peaches symbolize lush sensuality. Like fresh, ripe fruit, she blossomed for the feasting of men. She's played by Gong Li, widely regarded as one of the most beautiful women in Chinese film.

Sayuri, a spectacularly rare beauty with her unusual, translucent gray eyes, threatens Hatsumomo the moment she enters the okiya (geisha house) at just nine years old. With gray eyes, she is distinguished as an exotic creature, prized for features elevating her from the pack. Men often comment on her rare beauty, wanting to possess her as a stunning trinket for their collection. The gray eyes were a fabrication by Golden to make her even more enticing and ornamental, falling in line with the common practice of white male writers contorting and sexualizing images of Asian women. Ultimately, Sayuri becomes even more ravishing and clever than Hatsumomo, her value heightened by the currency of youth, eventually overtaking Hatsumomo in competition. It's a reminder that under the patriarchy, the most stunning and youthful woman always wins the crown. It also mirrors the dynamics of modeling and how Asiaphiles view Asian women: interchangeable and disposable.*

—

Like millions, I was a huge fan of the book (and film), glossing over the countless disturbing tidbits and the messaging. Instead, I lost myself in Sayuri's lavish transformation from lowly maid to Gion's most celebrated and spectacular geisha. The infighting between Sayuri and Hatsumomo paralleled the girl-world dynamics of my high school, and I immediately found a kindred spirit in the awkward young geisha named Pumpkin, who lives in their okiya. In the same way Hatsumomo takes Pumpkin under her wing, my high school bestie, Vanessa, turned me into her project.

There were few Asian Americans in popular media in the '90s, but Vanessa, with her oval face and a full-bodied mane of Pantene-glossy hair, was an ideal Korean beauty who could have easily posed for *Sports Illustrated* or graced the cover of *Cosmopolitan*. She moved languidly like a jaded princess, unconcerned about the passage of time. Not only was she flawless, but she was also tough and street-smart, often recounting stories of brawls with other girls.

---

* The white producers of the movie also treated Asian ethnicities as interchangeable. Chinese actresses Zhang Ziyi (Sayuri) and Gong Li (Hatsumomo) and Malaysian actress Michelle Yeoh (Mameha) played Japanese characters in the film.

"This bitch was mad dogging me at the pool hall the other day," she'd say. "I looked her in the eye and said, 'Why you staring bitch? Am I that damn beautiful?'" Her tales of tussles impressed me, having never gotten into a physical fight myself.

We grew up in Upland, a quiet suburb in Southern California's dusty, hot Inland Empire, located about an hour east of Los Angeles. It was a predominantly white city built in the foothills of the often snowcapped San Gabriel Mountains. Although the population was probably only about 4 percent Asian, Vanessa strutted through school as if she were prom queen and the locker lanes were her personal runway. I soaked in her rebellious spirit, an unconscious middle finger to the model minority stereotype—ditching class, hanging out with wannabe gangsters, and sneaking out at night. After befriending her, I embraced Asian American culture completely, dropping my white friends and hanging out with only Asians for the next fifteen years.

Vanessa and I were part of the "bad" Asian girls at Upland High School, but we were far from delinquent teenagers. We may have pined for the attentions of wannabe Asian gangsters from Wah Ching or Satanas, but our late-night excursions were tame, hanging out at Denny's, Asian cafés, pool halls, or karaoke rooms. Neither of us had leaned into our sexuality yet, and I graduated high school with my virginity intact, having hardly tasted alcohol, and never trying drugs.

At night, Vanessa drove south down California State Route 83—also known as Euclid Avenue, the main street running through the heart of Upland—to pick me up in her aunt's copper Oldsmobile. One night, she piloted me and one of her other followers, Jill, to an apartment complex in Hacienda Heights.

"We're going to meet up with these dudes, Simon and Kwan," Vanessa said, as Jill and I nodded obediently from the back seat. "I just want to smoke a blunt first," she explained.

Vanessa guided us up the stairs to a small studio, where Kwan sat perched on a swiveling office chair, wearing a wife beater that showed off sleeves of colorful tattoos and baggy jeans. A cigarette dangled from his mouth while he rolled a blunt. Vanessa mentioned offhandedly that Kwan had just gotten out of prison and was an active member of the Wah Ching gang. He appeared to be about twenty-five years old and seemed tightly wound, an undertone of rage in his demeanor.

"Sit anywhere," said Simon, a lanky, handsome Thai guy of about twenty-one.

No other chairs were available, so Jill and I sat compliantly on the ground as Vanessa nestled onto the bed and took a hit off the joint the guys were passing around.

Simon nodded in our direction. "Take a hit."

Jill and I demurred; we had never tried drugs before. We were mostly silent as Vanessa and Simon caught up, but in the presence of strange boys, our femininity took on a hallowed sheen of importance. The boys noticed us too as they became increasingly stoned, pupils dilating into dead black holes. Eventually, Simon sidled up to Jill, and Kwan edged onto the floor beside me.

"You have beautiful eyes," he said, squinting at my face with breath skunking of weed.

This attention from a much older man was novel and welcome, yet layered with an icky warning buzz, which I shoved to the side. Instead, I smiled and blushed. Suddenly, his lips were on me as he pushed me onto the floor. I glanced to the side and saw that Jill was already kissing Simon. My kiss with Kwan was unexpected, and I felt simultaneously queasy and something adjacent to pleasure. Aside from a quick, slurpy peck, it was my first real kiss. However, once he reached inside my shirt to my bra, I jumped away, giggling nervously. My massive insecurity about my flat chest saved things from going further. Otherwise, I might have been too meek to object.

As I squirmed away, my eyes caught Vanessa's. She said nothing, smiling wanly at me. The queen bee sat on an office chair throne, smoking as her girlfriends made out with guys around her. It was as if she were a mama-san, and we were her minion geisha to pimp out. In return, she gained status as the laid-back, cool girl, always down for the boys. Vanessa's friendship had ulterior motives. She'd enveloped several Upland girls into her transformational sphere, but they all ceased being friends with her after about six months (as I did eventually). Vanessa was the unabashed main character in her story, and we were just her willingly controlled puppets, ornaments enhancing her notoriety. Because of us, Vanessa gained popularity around Southern California's Asian community as a centerfold with a harem of attractive girlfriends—*harem* being the operative word. She offered up her friends as though they were playthings for the pleasure of men.

Channeling Vanessa and hanging out with her meant attention from boys, and that was the only validation I needed. While high school boys ignored me, they worshipped luminous Vanessa, whose paper phonebook overflowed with single Asian guys from Upland to Koreatown in LA to Orange County. Nobody asked me to homecoming or prom, but I went because Vanessa always set me up.

For our junior year homecoming dance, she found me a blind date. His name was Danny, a sophomore at nearby Etiwanda High School. I spent hours daydreaming of the big night, thinking of the one photo Vanessa showed me. I imagined he'd greet me with flowers, and I'd be swept off my feet by this six-foot-tall Korean boy with golden tan skin and spiky gelled hair. He'd open the passenger-side door for me and wave me into his lowered purple Honda Civic.

We got ready at Vanessa's house. She lived with her aunt and brother above 18th Street in a wealthier neighborhood than our modest one on 15th Street (the farther north you drive in Upland, the wealthier the families). They were the only Asian kids in Upland raised by their aunt—rare in our tiny Asian community. Vanessa never mentioned her parents. Her aunt became that "cool mom" who'd drive us to the mall and give opinions on our clothing and makeup. She seemed younger than the other Asian moms, with long wavy hair and a pretty but hardened face. Vanessa's aunt let her drive the family car and stay out as late as she wanted, and homecoming was no exception.

Vanessa styled my hair, flared with hairspray-shellacked bangs. She painted my face, penciling in my nonexistent eyebrows. Back then, the style was that of Asian American wannabe gangster girls, which appropriated fashion from Mexican cholas. We plucked off our eyebrows and drew them back in with a thin line. The look was completed with faces dunked in white foundation and powder, lips lined with a conspicuous ring of brown lip liner filled in with MAC Spice lipstick.

My strappy floral dress from Wet Seal was Vanessa's favorite pick from our mall trip. Because I was completely flat chested, I wore it with a pushup bra, squeezing nothing into lumps of something. My excitement sparked as I waited to meet my Korean prince. But it was anticlimactic; Danny barely spoke or looked at me on the drive over or at the dance itself. I was painfully shy, and he made zero effort. We didn't slow dance to the harmonized voices of Boyz II Men or All-4-One. Instead, we tailed Vanessa the entire night.

Vanessa found dances uncool; for her, they were merely photo ops. We dashed into line immediately upon arriving to get professional photos taken in our dresses and suits. Under the blinding lights, Danny and I posed awkwardly. The photographer instructed him to place his hands around my waist as my pulse fluttered. After our photo shoots were complete, our group of three couples left—in and out in approximately thirty minutes. The resulting pictures were exchanged weeks later like trading cards.

We fought the dry, howling Santa Ana desert winds back to the cars, no longer worried about messing up our meticulously curled hair. Some locals believe that these fabled winds, which can reach speeds upward of seventy-five miles per hour, dovetail with an increase in crime and negative feelings. These winds blasted so hard on occasion that Malibu and other parts of LA would sometimes spontaneously burst into flames. That night, the winds were relatively light, but they still blew away any chance at my fairy-tale ending with Danny.

After ditching the dance, we took the I-10 West to the 57 to the 60 into Hacienda Heights, one of the first distinct Chinese/Taiwanese neighborhoods in eastern San Gabriel Valley. Here, Asian American families achieved the dream of suburban home-ownership, also crowding the surrounding cities of Diamond

Bar, Rowland Heights, and Walnut. Developers sold buyers on a country aesthetic, a romanticized and white-adjacent style of living, shielded from the dangers of urban life and paving the path to assimilation. It was a perfectly monotonous immigrant dream of desirable school districts, Kumon classes, Saturday Chinese language schools, and tract housing with rectangular lawns of automatic sprinkler–watered Bermuda grass.

For us teenagers, it was the promised land of Asian American belonging, dotted with strip malls stuffed with Chinese grocery stores, Hong Kong–style barbecue restaurants, and shaved ice desserts. We came for boba and karaoke, and Danny spent the night teasing Vanessa. He poured her drinks and lit her cigarettes, offering me none. At the end of the night, Vanessa playfully jumped onto his back, and Danny piggybacked her through the parking lot until he tossed her off gently to admonish her after she dared to tap at his perfectly gelled and spiked hair. I seethed, ignored and forgotten, trailing behind in the wake of their unabashed flirtations. After getting home that night, I soaked in a scalding bath, dunking my head underwater. I wanted to evaporate and disintegrate into a million pieces like my jasmine-scented bath bomb, to disappear down the drain and into the sea.

Danny didn't call me after the dance. I wasn't surprised, but I was devastated to hear he later called me ugly and cross-eyed.

———

Memoirs of a Geisha confirmed all my misguided beliefs about female rivalries, feminine worth (or the lack of), and outer appearances. The book affirmed that pursuing glamour was not just worthwhile, it was required—something I'd already learned from my brief friendship with Vanessa. It reinforced the belief that we had to compete to reach some kind of imagined promised land, offering our bodies to men for renown. Being the most stunning meant men would elevate my status and gift me with jewels to make my sparkle even brighter. To me, it proved we needed to be seductive to captivate men. It was the only way, I thought, to make sure I wouldn't dissolve into a ghost. If I couldn't pleasure men, I was worthless.

I read the book as though it were a guide on the art of seduction, gleaning every painstaking detail about a geisha's makeup routine, her coy mannerisms, and the way her sultry eyes glimmered. I desperately wished I could emulate the power illustrated in one iconic scene, where Mameha, Sayuri's geisha mentor, explains that a woman's eyes are the most expressive part of her body: "You cannot call yourself a true geisha until you can stop a man in his tracks with a single look," she says to Sayuri.

Mameha demonstrates, flicking her eyes toward a man and sending a magnetic jolt of interest before looking away quickly. In a simple pink kimono, spare makeup, and red bow–topped hair, Sayuri practices this new skill on a bike-riding boy. He is so mesmerized he crashes into a truck, knocking chickens clucking to the ground. I wished I had that superpower. I'd never had that talent. *Where do women even learn to flirt?* I wondered. *Does it just come naturally to some?* I read that scene repeatedly, hoping to master the secrets of geisha, forgetting the book was written by a white man who had no idea of a geisha's true inner life.

For all of Golden's lack of knowledge, the book is written in the first person, as if it were a historical, autobiographical text.

What's even more troubling is that, according to Kimiko Akita, in her 2006 essay, "Orientalism and the Binary of Fact and Fiction in *Memoirs of a Geisha*," literature and humanities classes in the United States study the novel, further cementing the fictional novel as historical text. The book is little more than a bit of highly entertaining Orientalist fluff, an exotic fantasy romanticizing female subjugation, framed as a tell-all revealing the unknowable secrets of the elusive Asian woman. While geisha are rare (most Japanese have never met one), some Westerners believe that Japan is filled with geisha selling sex. This common Western association of geisha with prostitutes is erroneous. In truth, geisha from top okiya rarely slept with customers. They were in fact talented artists, musicians, singers, and dancers, yet the misconception permeates our understanding of geisha.

That geisha are artists is in the word itself. Gei means "art," and sha, "person," but both Golden's book and its movie adaptation obsess more over their physicality. Instead of leading with her artistry, under the Western male gaze, the geisha becomes an ornamental sex toy. Much time in both the book and film is spent on a geisha's transformative three-hour makeup routine, painstakingly lacquered and maintained hair, lush silk kimonos—and her resulting hypnotic power over men. Almost half the film is dedicated to the strategic sale of Sayuri's virginity in mizuage, a fictionalized ceremony marking the coming of age of a young geisha. In the movie and book, it's misrepresented as a graduation for apprentice geisha ready to entertain and perform. In Golden's world, one isn't a full geisha until one has sold off her virginity. Sayuri's virginity makes history with the highest-ever winning bid during her mizuage.

However, the sexual aspect of a geisha's graduation ceremony is heavily disputed by many geisha. To start, Mineko Iwasaki, the primary source of inspiration for *Memoirs of Geisha*, hated the book and Golden's detailing of mizuage.* Mineko describes her own mizuage in her memoir, *Geisha: A Life*, as a round of formal visits announcing her graduation and presenting gifts to other geisha houses and important patrons—not as a deflowering virginity sale. She asserts that the sexual aspect of mizuage never happened in Gion. Another geisha named Teruko told *The New York Times* that when giving lectures about geisha life at Columbia University in 1998, "all the questions from the students were about this book. . . . They wanted to know when I had my mizuage, how much was paid and what the sex was like." Most people came away from the book and movie focused on the idea that geisha are prostitutes and courtesans.† That fact highlights the film as nothing more than a gorgeously shot $85 million Asian fetish fantasy focusing on Asian women's submissive yet voracious sexuality.

Even as a virgin when reading the book, the internal message—that Asian women are only good for sex—seemed clear. Much like how Vanessa pimped me and other girls out to boys, Golden's

---

* After the book's publication, in 2001, Iwasaki sued Golden for a portion of the book's profits, alleging defamation. She claimed he destroyed her reputation in the geisha community and reneged on an agreement to keep her identity secret.

† Prostitutes often wore geisha attire and makeup to attract customers, which may have led some to believe that real, trained geisha were selling sex. Either way, after the Prostitution Prevention Law of 1956, prostitution was abolished.

geisha fantasy affirmed that an Asian woman's worth lay only in her ability to please men. The more men worshipped her, the more valuable she was. These misconceptions were further emphasized by a scene in the film when Sayuri, Pumpkin, and Sayuri's beloved Chairman are in an onsen (a hot spring) with American soldiers after the war. As the group climbs out of the springs, the much older American colonel pulls Sayuri aside for a private conversation.

"So, what is the protocol . . . Suppose I wanted to see you in private," he asks.

She responds indignantly, refusing the offer, but he crowds her into a corner, placing his large paw on her naked shoulder, asking for her price. Sayuri is offended by his unabashed assumption he could use her as a prostitute, an exotic balm for his homesickness. Then one of Sayuri's clients, Nobu, confronts her as she exits the pool. "Just the idea of you with him, with any man, you would be dead to me!" he screams. He reveals that his hope is to be Sayuri's danna, or patron. When she demurs, he talks down at her fervently. "I will not be refused . . . I do not like things held up before me that I cannot have."

Sayuri later concocts an elaborate plan to deter Nobu forever, as she's in love with his good friend and business partner, the Chairman. She seduces the colonel she just rejected, appearing in transparent robes in his bedroom and allowing him to remove her clothing and kiss her body. These conjoined scenes present two conflicting messages about an Asian woman's sexuality. Initially, Sayuri rejects the colonel, gaining momentary autonomy. Later, as she makes him her pawn, using her body as a strategic tool, it's another moment of twisted empowerment, but only because her body becomes a weapon. In Golden's geisha fantasy, sex is the geisha's most valuable currency, the defining component in her limited power arsenal. In his tale, told through a white male lens, Asian women are born for sex.

The millions of readers and viewers exposed to geisha for the first time through Golden's bestselling book and its highly successful on-screen adaptation were taught about a secretive Japanese world where women submit to compete for male attention and sexual validation. It's not absurd for male viewers to extrapolate from the film and other Orientalist media that all Asian women behave similarly. The idea that all Asian women are sex-crazed like geisha is one of the most disproportionately represented stereotypes. (There are at least two recently published books about how to seduce a man like a geisha. One of the books recommends teaching yourself how to squirt [female ejaculate] to please your man.)

I witnessed this misconception firsthand later during my modeling and acting career. Men often offered to be my sugar daddy, like the geisha-danna relationship promoted by Golden. A magazine mogul offered me a monthly allowance and a fancy apartment in exchange for sexual availability. Another decades older movie producer who claimed he'd launched the careers of several known actresses promised to do so for me. All I needed to do was become his sexual plaything and exotic armpiece to events, and he'd shower me with fame, beautiful clothing, cash, and expensive dinners. It wasn't my nature to be flirty with any of these men, but they still offered me such opportunities because, to them, I appeared to be a dumb, compliant doll like one of Golden's geisha.

Golden's geisha fantasy has its roots in sexual slavery and subjugation. He writes, in Sayuri's voice, "All the stories about invading American soldiers raping and killing us had turned out to be wrong; and in fact, we gradually came to realize that the Americans on the whole were remarkably kind." This ridiculously erases the fact that as American forces poured into Japan in 1945, the local governments quickly set up "comfort stations" (essentially on-site brothels filled with Japanese prostitutes or recruits) for the troops. These women had to service fifteen to sixty soldiers a day and described the sex with American GIs as ghastly and animalistic. According to translated documents reviewed by the Associated Press, the Ibaraki Prefectural Police Department wrote, "The strategy was, through the special work of experienced women, to create a breakwater to protect regular women and girls." In short, if comfort stations were unavailable, American soldiers would rape local women instead. This became a real issue when the Recreation and Amusement Association's comfort station in Tokyo shut down because of rampant venereal disease spread by soldiers. After its closing, reported rapes of local women rose from 40 to 330 daily, according to John Dower in his book *Embracing Defeat: Japan in the Wake of World War II*.

Beyond World War II, American forces also invaded several other Asian countries and prostituted Asian women along the way. During the Philippine-American War in 1889–1902, the idea that Filipina women were "little brown fucking machines powered by rice" grew roots. According to the film scholar Celine Parreñas Shimizu, this phrase was so recognizable that you could find street vendors hawking T-shirts and hats with the acronym LBFM near U.S. military bases. Here and in other occupied Asian countries, women could be bought for the price of a cigarette. The abundance of sexually available women was used by the American military to boost morale and help soldiers recover from battlefield trauma. "After soldiers spent several months fighting in the war, the military sent them off for R&R in Tokyo, Seoul, Hong Kong, Taipei, Manila, Bangkok, Kuala Lumpur, Singapore, and Hawaii," Kimberly Kay Hoang says in *Dealing in Desire: Asian Ascendancy, Western Decline, and the Hidden Currencies of Global Sex Work.* "In each of these locales, hundreds of nightclubs, massage parlors, and bathhouses lined the streets, featuring local female entertainers awaiting the arrival of American GIs." Asian American studies professor Josephine Park in Angela Huang and Arina McGinn's article "Dating While Asian at Penn" further emphasizes the misogyny, citing how soldiers joked that R&R stood for rape and restitution.

Then, of course, there's the "me so horny" line from a famous scene in Stanley Kubrick's 1987 hit movie about the Vietnam War, *Full Metal Jacket* (which earned $120 million at the box office). Although most today have not seen the movie, they're likely familiar with the indelible phrase from the film "me so horny, me love you long time." This one sentence alone has been a major driving force in perpetuating the hypersexual Asian woman archetype while making Asian women the butt of the joke. Just two years later, 2 Live Crew rapped it permanently into popular culture by co-opting the derogatory phrase as the title and refrain for their 1989 hit song. They rocketed "me so horny, me love you long time" into the stratosphere. As clubbers laughed and danced to the earworm's beat, they did so at our expense, trampling our dignity. Today, American soldiers no longer wage wars in Asian countries, but the stink of the ideology pressed on Asian women by the U.S. military persists.

After the Vietnam War, millions of tourists from the United

States and Europe visited Thailand in the 1990s for its sex industry, initially built for American troops. According to "White Sexual Imperialism: A Theory of Asian Feminist Jurisprudence," by Sunny Woan, in the early 1990s, Thailand had seven million tourists. Solitary male travelers composed an estimated 65 percent of that number, and 70 percent of those single men came for sex. That means in one year alone, approximately 4.9 million men visited Thailand for sex tourism. Almost fifty years after the Vietnam War, men are still pouring into countries like Thailand to reap the benefits of past colonization efforts.

Along with Golden's erroneous depiction of geisha, Western male sex tourism to Asian countries bolsters the oversexed and always-willing Asian woman stereotype, which was splashed across television and movie screens in the late 1990s and early 2000s. As a young woman, I took these influences at face value, convinced that beauty and my body were commodities, actual currencies to exchange for joy and victory. I remember laughing, reading Vanessa's sign-off in my sophomore yearbook. She wrote in her signature artistic cursive, "I know you'll be rich or at least a trophy wife 2 a rich man that will beat u up!" Her message was an inside joke but read like a prophecy: being gorgeous would be an effortless main line to triumph and prosperity.

I wasn't bold enough yet to seduce like on-screen geisha or capitalize on my sexuality for male interest. My tiger mom's watchful gaze also made it hard to do so. But I gradually transformed myself at night when Vanessa and I would sneak out to rendezvous with Wah Ching and Satanas boys. Bit by bit, I learned to lean into my sexuality.

Although I never spoke to Vanessa again after high school, her influence, combined with *Memoirs of a Geisha,* taught me that we were playing a zero-sum game to win the patriarchy's spotlight—desirability dictated survival. Asian women, in particular, were bound to stringent and reductive beauty standards; we were prostituted symbols of desire, our sexuality commodified and fetishized.

BUTTERFLY

I was a sophomore in high school when I discovered Asian American pinup model Sung-Hi Lee and her titillating butterfly tattoo. That tattoo haunted me. As a little girl I had prayed to be beautiful. But I didn't pray to God; I prayed to a little caterpillar named Furry, and Sung-Hi's butterfly tattoo instantly reminded me of her.

Around our family home in the quiet suburb of Upland, California, dainty, furry black caterpillars dotted our herbaceous green bushes. One spring day while still in elementary school, I spotted a bright yellow one, her tiny form blooming in golden floss. She was extraordinary, a solitary platinum blonde in a sea of brunettes. To me she was like Tinker Bell, the shimmering fairy in Peter Pan's Neverland. I coaxed the trusting creature onto my pointer finger. My heart gleamed at the thought of making her mine. Her little feet tickled my finger, at first with featherlight touches, before desperately clinging on after realizing she was trapped.

I named the unwitting creature Furry and imprisoned her in a dark cardboard box, plucking her from the lush maze of the garden and putting her into solitary confinement. I wanted to nurture her into a butterfly, but days later, my Lhasa Apso, Puffy, bounded into my room and smashed the box—and the little caterpillar's side. Furry was left with a small bruise, which grew until it turned her entire body an ugly shade of violet. She died shortly after. My brother and I had a solemn burial ceremony, and I prayed for her little caterpillar soul nightly in apology. Years later, I continued to appeal to Furry, but my requests grew selfish.

"Grant me one wish," I beseeched my victim. "Make me bloom like a butterfly into the most beautiful girl in the world so every guy falls madly in love with me." I was nothing—unseen and completely unremarkable. I wanted to be like her, the golden caterpillar in a sea of black.

Discovering Sung-Hi felt like kismet, as though Furry had finally given me a sign, showing me the path to beauty. That year, Sung-Hi was at the height of her internet fame, with twelve total appearances in *Playboy*, and she was the first Asian model ever to grace the cover. Hundreds of fan sites on GeoCities (an early web hosting provider that allowed anyone to create and publish websites for free) praised her beauty. Her fans (predominantly white men) dubbed her "the Korean butterfly," a moniker referencing the delicate artwork above her naughty bits. The little orange-and-black butterfly sat daintily on her pelvis, wings folded up in flight, as if it were waving hello to her legion of followers, inviting them to consume her body and revel in her beauty.

The butterfly is especially prominent in her iconic photo for *Playboy Special Edition*. Like the famous Got Milk? ads of the nineties, which inspired the portrait, Sung-Hi holds a glass of milk delicately in her right hand, wearing a milk mustache over her top lip. That's where the similarities end. Lee's back is arched and she's entirely nude, save for thigh-high white stockings. Her famously inviting tattoo is highlighted by artfully dribbled rivulets of milk crisscrossing down her tanned body, running from her chest to the tips of the butterfly's wings.

The photo simulates a post–blow job and cum shot scene, depicting what many sex experts agree to be complete male domination with implied undertones of violence. This physical act of marking one's territory symbolizes ownership and supremacy, furthering the idea that Asian females are easily exploitable, obedient dolls. The drips of milk traversing down her body work in tandem with the butterfly tattoo to mark her—that body part in particular—as an object for male pleasure.

———

The day I discovered Sung-Hi's photos, I was goofing off in the middle of a lab assignment, as usual, bored with the test tubes before me and letting my partner do the bulk of the work, when my friend Sam sauntered over to my desk to share his recent discovery.

"Yo, check this out," he exclaimed, tossing a club flyer onto my desk. "I think I'm in love with her." Sam sighed, almost visibly salivating. "She's my dream girl."

"We're not old enough to go to this," I replied, rolling my eyes at his palpable desperation as I examined the glossy card. A stunning Asian woman clad in a shiny gold bikini gazed back at me from the page with a knowing glint in her eyes. This woman was a literal goddess—the most striking woman I had ever seen—while we were a pair of skinny teenagers living in possibly the dullest city in Southern California. Her voluminous black hair sat atop her head like a crown, cascading around her delicate heart-shaped face, framing achingly full lips and porcelain skin, while mine fell flatly against my too-long face. With her tiny button nose, her face was the kind of flawless that twists men's minds into losing reason, while my broad nose disqualified me from being considered beautiful in SoCal and my ancestral home of Taiwan. Sung-Hi Lee was desired by men worldwide; boys in Upland never even asked me out.

At the time, I spent my days dreaming about Steven, a beautiful rocker with long platinum-blond hair, stylish enough to pull off a color-blocked poncho but intelligent enough to be in my Advanced Placement English class. "He could be the Axl Rose to my Erin Everly," I gushed to my friend, glancing at Steven from across the classroom, hoping he'd make eye contact. He didn't.

One day, as I walked through the halls with Guns N' Roses' "Welcome to the Jungle" blasting in my headphones, I decided to let my feelings be known. I was too shy to tell him myself. Instead, I whispered about my crush to a mutual friend, hoping he'd spread the word. But instead of reciprocating my feelings, Steven blurted out loudly for the whole class to hear, "Ew, that dog is in love with me?" My first public humiliation confirmed my deepest fear: *I was undesirable.* The feeling has never entirely gone away. After that, I became convinced that women like me, with dark hair and eyes, could never be considered beautiful. The popular girls in school were the blondest girls with crystalline blue eyes. These girls were the type who grew up to be models and movie stars, while I didn't make the cut.

I idolized supermodels like Cindy Crawford, Claudia Schiffer, and Christy Turlington, wishing I resembled them, though impossible. They were white and curvy in all the ways I wasn't. I subscribed to the Victoria's Secret catalog, with nary an Asian model featured, despite having no intention of purchasing lingerie because I had nothing to show off. Flipping through the pages admiring models in their barely there lingerie, I imagined myself in their shoes, hardly registering how absurdly sexualized the photos were for a publication geared toward women. The models were occasionally topless, though the catalog tried to sell bras. It was basically soft porn.

I devoured the *Sports Illustrated: The Making of the Swimsuit Issue* specials, watching the world's most renowned models traverse far-flung destinations wearing the tiniest of bikinis—or less. In awe, I watched as all-American golden girl Rachel Hunter— the tanned blond Amazonian wife of rock star Rod Stewart— minxed for the *Sports Illustrated* 1993 calendar, wishing it were me shining brilliantly on camera. Her arms stretched long above her head, and her eyes were trained on the camera with a sultry stare. A thin sliver of soapy bubbles barely covered her nipples while she carefully kept the shower water streaming down her back—a single drop of water in front would leave her fully exposed. I even purchased Crawford's *Shape Your Body Workout* tape and followed along to Crawford herself holding on to the back of a chair and swinging her gazelle legs while Seal sang in the background: "But we're never gonna survive, unless we get a little crazy." *Seal is right*, I'd think, as I aped Crawford's graceful movements. Was it so crazy to hope her secrets would lend me a bit of supermodel sheen?

After school the day Sam showed me that flyer, I clamored to use our family desktop computer when I got home. Back then, it took an entire two minutes and thirty seconds for the dial-up internet to load. Following the dial tone was a litany of melodious punches on a telephone keypad, until, finally, the loud, cacophonous belch of beeps and static indicated connection to the web. The desperate hope was always that no one would call, knocking me off the internet and requiring the process to start all over again. I typed "Sung-Hi Lee" into Yahoo! Search, the preferred internet search platform of the '90s, and became instantly obsessed.

I was particularly entranced by her Got Milk? photo and the way it enhanced her tattoo. I stared at the photo repeatedly over the next few years, wishing it were me clutching that glass of milk on camera. I found her tattoo edgy but elegant, not understanding that it could be seen as self-objectification. Sung-Hi likely didn't realize it either. On her website, she explained she loved butterflies for their beauty and metamorphosis, feeling like a butterfly herself. But even if her fascination was innocent, it's unlikely her legion of fans saw anything beyond a sexual similarity between her and her body art.

Butterflies are renowned for their loveliness. They are also elegant, fragile little works of art, easily captured and vulnerable to objectification. As a child, I read the short story "The Collector," written by J. B. Stamper. In the dark tale, a teenage boy is fascinated with butterflies and moths and kills them to pin as trophies for display. Later, he is swarmed by giant moths and disappears. He's later found pinned to a tree himself. The most troubling part of that story is that it highlights the centuries-long practice in lepidopterology (the scientific study of butterflies and moths) of collecting and killing live specimens of these winged creatures. The process can be gruesome, using such instruments as a potassium cyanide–infused killing jar, razor-sharp metal pins, and diaphanous nets, among others. Beyond scientists, there are scores of children and adults collecting butterflies for their personal enjoyment.

Asiaphiles, too, have a history of "collecting" Asian women, using them as masturbation material or cum vessels before carelessly tossing one aside for another. It's one of the most enduring stereotypes about Asian women, rooted in war and oppression. Much like the "comfort stations" provided during wars abroad that normalized the prostitution and rape of Asian women, the butterfly trope has roots in similar practices during U.S. occupation in Asian countries. And like butterflies violently murdered and pinned to walls for display, there's a direct correlation between fetishization and violence, something we witnessed firsthand with the 2021 spa shootings in Atlanta.

The Asian butterfly trope became mainstream starting with the 1922 film *The Toll of the Sea*, starring Anna May Wong and based on Giacomo Puccini's 1904 opera, *Madama Butterfly*, still one of the world's most widely performed and renowned operas. The source of the opera, in turn, is said to be the 1887 novel *Madame Chrysanthème*, the French writer Pierre Loti's loosely autobiographical story of a naval officer who takes a temporary child-wife—a "little, creamy-skinned woman with black hair and cat's eyes"—when visiting Nagasaki. After he meets his wife, Chrysanthème, he says, "What thoughts are running through that little brain? . . . [I]t is a hundred to one that she has no thoughts whatever. And even if she had, what do I care?"

We continue to see the ideology of *Madama Butterfly* underscored in popular culture to this day. For example, Rivers Cuomo, the lead singer of Weezer, named the band's 1996 hit record *Pinkerton*, after the male lead in *Madama Butterfly*. It's widely regarded as one of the greatest albums of the 1990s, with lyrics based on Cuomo's life. One song titled "Butterfly" is about him capturing his own "butterfly." He sings about not meaning to do the "butterfly" any harm, unable to resist his own male bodily urges.

In an interview with half-Japanese journalist Clare Kleinedler for *Addicted to Noise*, Cuomo describes Pinkerton as a character he can relate to, the ultimate male id who goes to Japan and has sex with a fifteen-year-old Japanese girl, impregnates her, and abandons her. "He's thoroughly despicable. [long pause] But I can't deny that there's some of that in me," Cuomo says, likely referring to his many "disastrous encounters with Asian girls of all sorts," which he mentions earlier in the interview. It's an odd interview, as though he were simultaneously apologizing for having an Asian fetish and loudly proclaiming it. Regardless of his intentions, his lyrics seem to normalize the colonialist association between Asian women and butterflies.

The core of *Madama Butterfly* and *The Toll of the Sea* is a story inspired by an early seventeenth-century practice in which Japanese pimps offered newly arrived foreigners a prostitute for the duration of their trip. These were considered a temporary "marriage," which could be ended by the "husband" at any time. The only difference between *Madama Butterfly* and *The Toll of the Sea* is that the film takes place in China instead of Japan. The same premise would be adapted for Vietnam during the Vietnam War in *Miss Saigon*. In each, the men feel free to statutorily rape under-age girls—just fifteen years old in *Madame Chrysanthème*—and unceremoniously discard them afterward.

Lotus Flower, the protagonist in *The Toll of the Sea*, is a victim of grooming, desperately in love with a much older man who abuses her and then leaves her, returning to America to marry a white woman. Years later, he's back in China with his wife, Beatrice, and Lotus Flower has been waiting for him this entire time—with their toddler son. Upon learning of Beatrice, she gives the couple her son and commits suicide by tossing herself into the ocean. *Madama Butterfly* and *Miss Saigon* end similarly. In all these versions of the same enduring story about Asian women written by white men, the Asian women all enact self-inflicted violence on themselves—highlighting the fragility of butterflies. The Asian butterfly is the ultimate self-sacrificial lamb in the patriarchal male fantasy, allowing herself to be captured and used however the man pleases. Much like the ease of killing butterflies to decorate our walls, she is killed and discarded when her ornamental appearance no longer elicits pleasure.

Fans of butterflies like Sung-Hi and me (after I became a model) collected our photos and calendars, hanging them up as masturbation decor, imagining what being with an Asian woman would be like, projecting their fantasies onto our image. We weren't people. We were naked placeholders, living embodiments of exoticness. Over the course of my modeling career, I'd wonder: Did my fans realize I had dreams that didn't involve staring up at them nude and wide-eyed on a silk bedsheet? Did they know or even care that my favorite ice cream flavor is vanilla? That I adored fluffy animals and fatalistic druggie movies? I doubt it. My fans likely infused me with whatever personality they desired. I was a blank slate for their fantasies. A follower once wrote to me, "Chatting with you and meeting you is why I have an Asian wife"— something I've heard countless times before. At first glance, it reads as a compliment, like I should be tickled I inspired him to procure an Asian lover. Upon deeper consideration, the inspiration I had on his choice of a wife had to be purely physical. Unlike fans of celebrities who often attempt to learn details about their idols' lives in hopes of forming a parasocial relationship, my fans rarely engaged me in any sort of deep conversation, not regarding me as an autonomous being and treating me like a collectible postage stamp. That fan's comment illustrates this perfectly. I'll bet his wife and I share very few personality traits, if any at all. But that doesn't matter, because I doubt we ever had a conversation long enough for him to decide that my temperament embodied the characteristics he wanted in a partner. There's no space for the reality of an Asian woman's personhood to muddy an Asiaphile's personal fantasies of Asian female conquests.

—

Sung-Hi was the first Asian model I saw, and discovering her, hope sprang that I could one day be like Crawford and the models gracing my precious Victoria's Secret catalogs. Staring into Sung-Hi's eyes on my computer screen, the puzzle pieces of desirability fused together. I vowed never to be seen as a "dog" again and started to believe that the only way I could be seen as beautiful was to play the role of a stereotypical object of desire. Sung-Hi was the first woman described as beautiful who looked like me, and she had to bare herself to the world to earn that description. The pretty girls on television—Jennifer Aniston, Sarah Michelle Gellar, and Jennie Garth—and the popular girls in school were white women whose features looked nothing like mine.

When I revealed my true feelings and my crush found me disgusting, I subconsciously concluded that Asian women like Sung-Hi and me didn't get ahead by revealing our authentic selves. We were desirable only when sexualized and bending to the whims of men. My new dream was to become an internet goddess and grace the cover of *Playboy*, just like Sung-Hi. I started collecting her calendars and *Playboy*s and joined her website. I decided that I had no qualms about shedding my clothing. If she could do it, so could I.

Slowly, I morphed. I incorporated Sung-Hi's smoky eyeshadow and overlined plump lips, paired with formfitting tank tops and tight jeans, into my look when I snuck out at night to hang with Asian wannabe gangster boys. I would even change my name, but that would come later.

No one would be interested in the real me, I thought, and so, over several years, I systematically erased anything authentically me.

ABGs

In college, I had a twin of sorts—Cherise from San Gabriel High School—only she was prettier and more voluptuous. I first learned about her my junior year of high school. Being from San Gabriel, located about fourteen miles east of Los Angeles, she was instantly edgier by default. San Gabriel was one of a cluster of cities, including Monterey Park, Alhambra, and Arcadia, formerly known as the first suburban Chinatown. Starting in the 1970s, Fred Hsieh, a Chinese Realtor, marketed the area as the "Chinese Beverly Hills," and Chinese and Taiwanese flocked to the area over several decades for its respectable school district, brand-new affordable homes, and proximity to Los Angeles. In 1995, a *Los Angeles Times* columnist dubbed the area the "nation's Chinese food capital."

On weeknights, I'd sneak out of my parents' house to meet my twenty-one-year-old Alhambra-based Chinese boyfriend, Jimmy, who'd whisk me from my boring white suburb to the Hong Kong–

style café St. Honore in Monterey Park. Dating a much older man meant automatic street cred, but it's disturbing now to consider why this twenty-one-year-old was driving two hours round trip to Upland to hang out with fifteen-year-old me. Back then, I proudly rode shotgun in his navy-blue hatchback Civic, feeling badass as he slowly maneuvered over driveways at an angle to avoid scraping the bottom of his dropped car. Over sizzling plates of steak drenched with black pepper sauce and hot milk tea with thick jars of condensed milk on the side, one of Jimmy's friends would inevitably say, "You look just like this girl from San Gabriel named Cherise." I had no idea what she looked like, but whenever her name was brought up, I would instantly feel defensive and competitive. Who was this supposed twin? Was she better-looking than me?

To my surprise and horror, during my first week on campus at the University of California, San Diego (UCSD), I discovered my twin was also a freshman there. What were the odds? UCSD was divided into seven colleges, and to add insult to injury, Cherise was at Revelle—the smart kids' college—whereas I was at Muir—home of the slackers. I was called Cherise on more than one occasion, to which I'd reply icily, "I'm not her!" before rolling my eyes and stomping off.

When I finally saw Cherise in real life, I found her rather pretty but didn't believe we looked alike. She instantly became the it girl of UCSD's Asian American circles. Cherise was effortlessly confident. Gliding across campus, she walked with back arched and tits up, whereas I slouched, books clasped in front of my padded bra. One afternoon, I walked into the cafeteria wearing a black top emblazoned with dozens of violet Moschino monograms and saw Cherise at the table next to mine dressed elegantly in black boots, skinny jeans, and a formfitting black top.

"I'd never be so tacky as to wear something covered in logos," I overheard her say to her stylish but snarky friend Joseph, as they burst out laughing. I felt humiliated but knew she was aware that people thought we were twins and clearly also hated the comparisons.

A few weeks into my freshman year, she even bested me at my own game. A bunch of freshmen got together at San Diego's sole private karaoke room spot downtown. I'd spent countless hours karaoking in high school and was certain I could finally one-up Cherise, convinced I was superior in this department. But Cherise's song, Whitney Houston's "Saving All My Love for You," started playing before my song, Mariah Carey's "Hero." With a cigarette in her left hand, she casually belted out a killer version of Houston's hit. Feeling defeated, I left the room to smoke and skipped singing that night.

The worst part about Cherise was her C-cup breasts, making her, in my mind, instantly better. I was convinced that breasts were badges of femininity, and my A-cups didn't make the cut. I was never a tomboy, more the ultimate girlie girl, sugary pink and frilly as a tutu—girl squared. It was unfair.

Since my sophomore year in high school, I'd worn a padded bra, never letting any guy feel me up. I was extremely insecure about my nonexistent chest, hiding it from everyone, including my first college boyfriend, Jin, whom I met at a mixer during the first week of school. This boy was just my type: he was K-pop idol handsome with pale skin and dressed like an Asian gangster wannabe in a white shirt paired with sagged, baggy jeans and slicked back hair. When we first met, he fired off questions with a slight smile: "Are you a freshman? What college are you from?" I learned he was Teochew Chinese, from San Gabriel, and a sophomore majoring in computer sciences at Marshall College, located across the sprawling 2,178-acre campus from Muir. Jin seemed much more mature because he lived at the UCSD apartments, sharing a two-bedroom with his best friend, Ross, and two other sophomores. He left the party with my pager number, and I found myself in an instant relationship.

Our first date, the next day, was at the on-campus recreation center (neither of us had cars). All the Asian guys played pool, and he showed me how to aim the cue, crouching behind me and grasping my arms as if I were his marionette. I pretended to care so his hands would linger on me. After that, we were inseparable. He'd walk me to class every morning, and I ached for him whenever we were apart. It was my first experience with puppy love. The first time I went over to his apartment, he squeezed me tightly. Slightly tipsy, he whispered passionately, "I like you so much." I felt dazed with happiness, but it was tempered by self-consciousness over my padded bra.

I absolutely hated that I needed to hide my flat chest while Cherise flaunted her C-cup implants. She even brought several copies of a calendar she appeared in, handing them out to everyone. It quickly became the buzz around campus. Several guys, including my friend Brian, hung it in their dorm rooms. Cherise was Miss March, wearing tight black booty shorts and a crop top showing off ample cleavage. She stood confidently with her hip cocked and legs apart in front of a silver Nissan Skyline. That calendar also featured Daphne Kong from Pacific Rim Racing, the first import model to achieve fame in that community.

When I first saw Cherise's picture hanging in Brian's dorm, I scoffed in disgust and simultaneous envy. She looked great (though I refused to admit it), but the calendar quality was inferior compared with the glossy glitz of Sung-Hi's *Playboy* covers and calendars. It was like Forever 21 versus Versace, in different leagues. I never admitted how secretly jealous I was of how perky her breasts looked in the photos.

———

Asian women and import models with large breasts like Cherise's (and as I would have later) were part of an Asian American–created archetype called ABGs, short for "Asian baby girls" or "Asian baby gangsters," although the term didn't exist back then. Most attribute the popularization of the term to the Facebook group Subtle Asian Traits, also known as SAT. The ABG aesthetic refers to Asian women living in Western countries and was meant to be an act of resistance against the model minority myth. Although it later became a sexualized aesthetic, it didn't start that way. Chinese, Japanese, and Korean women have since appropriated this look, but the original teenagers inspiring the term were Vietnamese, Cambodian, or Laotian. Instead of immigrating to America on work visas, many came as refugees and were among the first members of California's Asian gangs. A 1989 article in the *Los Angeles Times* details Orange County's new female Asian gang problem. These young teenage girls not only fought with fists, but they were also armed with semiautomatic weapons and knives. "She has dyed amber hair, a knife-cut tattoo on her forearm that says 'I Love Tuan,' and a way of hunching her shoulders that tells adults to drop dead," wrote Sonni Efron. There was no mention of the teenagers acting sexy or being scantily clad.

As East Asians co-opted this look, it became sexified with bleached hair, hoop earrings, skimpy clothing, tattoos, eyelash extensions, and razor-sharp winged eyeliner. ABGs were considered high-maintenance. In addition to a boob job, an ABG had monthly nail, eyelash, and hair appointments to maintain her expensive and highly curated look. Rebelling against stereotypes, ABGs were tough, outgoing, and sexually empowered. You could find them on the passenger side of lowered Toyota MR2s and colorful Civics blasting songs from Jodeci and Boyz II Men.

The aesthetic both highlighted our femininity and empowered us to move beyond portrayals as weak and pathetic. We didn't realize we were appealing to Orientalist fantasies with our enhanced breasts, suggestively placed tattoos, exposed midriffs, and dangling belly button rings, dancing all night with aplomb, high on ecstasy at raves. This sexualized stereotype has become a battle between Eastern and Western expectations of women. ABGs value individuality and self-empowerment, in direct conflict with Eastern values of meekness and modesty. Heavily tied to physical appearance, this label continues to default to the male gaze, and although it flouts the fawning lotus flower and nerdy Asian stereotypes, it flattens and restricts those labeled as ABGs as caricatures, allowing them to be belittled and dismissed.

We see examples of this oversexed trope in *Mean Girls* (2004) through the Vietnamese high schoolers Trang Pak and Sun Jin

Dinh, who hook up with their gym teacher. The mean white girls in the movie called Trang a "grotsky little beotch" because she's caught making out with the unattractive and much older Coach Carr. It's of course a nod at the hypersexual Asian trope, with the two Asian girls as the butt of the joke since they are both fighting over the coach, who is actually a predator conducting statutory rape. There are also the scantily clad, lustful twins Fook Mi and Fook Yu in *Austin Powers in Goldmember* (2002) and all the sexy, silent ABGs in the Fast & Furious franchise. Like the geisha in Arthur Golden's novel, these characters all embody carnality.

The larger breasts from implants my generation of Asian women got were just icing on the cake. Asian women have smaller breasts on average as the result of a thirty-five-thousand-year-old gene mutation. Yet Western beauty standards influenced many of us to turn to breast augmentation to fit in with our more ample-chested white peers. Although I've never heard an Asiaphile complain about flat chests, fetishists benefited from this surgery—both physically and sexually.

It's arguable that without these bags of saline and silicone, an entire generation of Asian pinup models might not have existed, meaning millions of photos for Asian fetishists to beat off to wouldn't have been created. Every major import model of my generation had implants except for Natasha Yi and Sasha Singleton— both famously all-natural C-cups. Still, both got implants after gravity took its toll. Without question, implants were an essential component of my pinup journey. Without them, I wouldn't have dared.

Unknowingly, Asian pinup models with larger-than-natural breasts further perpetuated the Asian fetish, specifically the idea of Asian women as sex toys. Western beauty standards entered the equation even when Asian features were desired.

With her rebellious nature and breast-implant-enhanced sexuality, the ABG seems to be a variation on the more aggressive, Lucy Liu–esque dragon lady trope. Both ooze sex and are the opposite of the butterfly. But while the dragon lady is a powerful dominatrix, the ABG is a free-spirited wild child. Either way, Asian women can't escape being intrinsically tied to sex. In "The Asian Baby Girl (ABG) Through a Filipina American Lens," authors Stacey Anne Baterina Salinas and Talitha Angelica (Angel) Acaylar Trazo call the ABG stereotype just another variation on the hypersexualized Asian female tropes of the past and a modern-day "model minority girl nympho." In other words, even when we try to rebel against the wilting flower or delicate butterfly, Asian women are still diminished to a paper-thin, hypersexual image with no agency as multifaceted individuals. As Salinas and Trazo write, this is "a feat that no Asian woman can overcome within the systems of imperialism, racism, and heteropatriarchy."

———

By the time midterm season rolled around, I'd broken up with Jin. Ending relationships was a defensive coping mechanism for my abandonment issues. Instead of dealing with conflict, I'd leave before my boyfriends had the chance to dump me. It doubled as a test and opportunity for them to prove their love by chasing and begging for me back. Symptomatic of my deep-seated lack of self-worth, I felt safe only when aggressively pursued. Jin did not do this.

Instead, I mourned the breakup, playing R&B group Az Yet's cover of Chicago's "Hard to Say I'm Sorry" on repeat. Weeks later, as I slunk around, depressed at home for Christmas break, Jin texted, "MISS YOU." I yearned for him terribly but didn't respond, needing him to pursue harder. He didn't, and I never saw him again. On a campus with almost forty thousand students and thousands of classes and seven colleges, we never crossed paths.

As I marinated in an echo chamber of depressing breakup songs, I wondered if Jin let me go so easily because of my flat chest, my pathetic attempts to hide it, and our sexless relationship. Because of my reticence and deceit, our relationship could never progress. Would he have needed me desperately if I were more like Cherise, whose gravity-defying tits perched confidently on her chest with considerable cleavage and visibly erect nipples? Would he have begged me to stay? Worshipped me into feeling secure? I was sick of concealing my lack of curves and didn't want to hide it from another boyfriend. I always knew I wanted implants one day, but after seeing Cherise in person and breaking up with Jin, that desire took on a palatable urgency.

That summer, I finally took the leap. No one would notice, I figured, as I already wore a padded bra. I would return as a sophomore with a complete set of C-cups that seemed like they'd been there all along. I forced my mother into helping me pay for it, threatening to put it on my credit card. She agreed to release all the money she had been saving for me from childhood gifts and red envelopes from relatives under the condition that she choose the doctor.

At her coworker's recommendation, we went to Dr. Francis Sheng. We drove to Dr. Sheng's office in the heart of Beverly Hills, where we were greeted by the receptionist, an attractive Chinese woman in her late twenties with wavy black-brown hair and a face perfectly made up as to appear natural.

"Hi," she said to my mom in Chinese, "we spoke on the phone. Here are some forms for your daughter to complete. Make yourselves comfortable, and Dr. Sheng will see you shortly."

Within minutes, she ushered us into Dr. Sheng's office. Left alone to remove all my clothing, I donned a flimsy gown, open in front for easy access. I sat gingerly and nervously on top of the crisply papered examination chair.

"What can I do for you today?" asked Dr. Sheng, a middle-aged Chinese man with a kind demeanor.

"I want breast implants!" I exclaimed, pulling a crumpled photo of Sung-Hi from my purse. "Can you make them exactly like hers?"

Sung-Hi had breast implants that could pass for natural, a 33 B-cup—smaller than the more popular C-cup most women got. I always hated obvious implants and gravitated toward watching porn stars with perfect natural breasts.

"Oh, her doctor did great work!" exclaimed Dr. Sheng. He had a gentle, effeminate manner, making me instantly comfortable. "So, we'll make the incision at the bottom of the nipple," he explained, drawing a line on me with a black marker as I stared blankly at a spot on the white wall, carefully avoiding eye contact. "It'll leave a scar, but hardly noticeable."

He snapped a photo, told me to change, and left the room.

On surgery morning, having fasted for twelve hours, I eagerly woke early to get ready before my appointment. Freshly showered, I drove with my mom to Dr. Sheng's office. Upon arriving, the nurse handed me a simple white hospital gown to wear. I felt pure, as if undergoing a sacramental ritual. To me, that surgery was akin to baptism, a rebirth into the ideal body of femininity I coveted so intensely.

———

As I write this book, body positivity—the celebration of natural features and bodies of all shapes and sizes—is trending. Some might consider me anti-feminist for undergoing surgery. Back when I got implants, unrealistic beauty standards were the norm, and some feminists slammed the misogyny of plastic surgery. In her 1995 book, *Reshaping the Female Body: The Dilemma of Cosmetic Surgery,* feminist Kathy Davis considers cosmetic surgery to be an act of submission to the patriarchy. The late feminist scholar and philosopher Sandra Lee Bartky believed that modifying our bodies to live up to the media's crushing influence on culturally accepted beauty was a subconscious submission to men. And I agree there is some truth to that. It's innately disturbing to voluntarily allow yourself to be cut open and mutilated for the male gaze: the blade slicing into flesh to erase my natural self, tearing my skin and filling it with foreign, artificial parts for the appeal of men. It's violent. It's the intersection of internalized misogyny and self-hatred, propagated by my damaged self-esteem stemming from childhood. Yet there's a poetic resonance to cutting yourself open and spilling blood in an attempt to become incrementally beautiful, turning yourself into a live blow-up toy for men. Like an actual doll, all my parts were replaceable and modifiable. It's objectification at its very core.

Breast augmentation is so painful I needed to be knocked unconscious for the procedure. I knew well of the many inherent risks but didn't care, so focused on the outcome and transformation. Years before I had watched *Breast Men* (1997), a semibiographical, dark drama about the advent of the first silicone breast implants. It was a deeply ominous tale of breast augmentations gone wrong and the often horrifying side effects. But that never deterred me. On surgery day, I was fearless, excited even.

I don't remember much of my recovery, instead enjoying an endless haze of Vicodin, asleep with my newly manufactured tits in my childhood bedroom, my previous breasts erased from memory. I had hardly ever looked at them to begin with. These synthetic breasts felt like mine, as if these teardrops of fullness had always been part of me. That first year, they stood unusually high on my chest, rocky orbs jutting out from my spindly frame. Over the years, they have fallen to a natural shape, and I couldn't be more pleased.

I've always said the implants were for me, to fit better in clothing. This was partially true—probably mostly rationalization. Having larger breasts was a major boon to my self-worth, which hinged on male attention, the whipping of heads in my direction. The surgery was empowering, and I felt like an entirely different person, confident and voluptuously carnal.

During high school in the nineties, I was mesmerized, along with millions, by Pamela Anderson running in slow motion down a Southern California beach, her breasts practically bouncing out of her tiny red swimsuit. She was the all-American fantasy girl come to life. I also loved glam metal bands like Skid Row, Mötley Crüe, and Warrant. These musicians all dated women like Pamela

Anderson and Bobbie Brown—another blond centerfold and Anderson clone. Brown starred as the dream girl in Warrant's "Cherry Pie" music video, which was inescapable on MTV in the early '90s. Women like this cemented the idea of the raw, animalistic power of a voluptuous chest. We were fed the idea that great tits could launch an entire career. Media also bombarded us with WonderBra ads starring the busty platinum-blond runway model Eva Herzigová. Next to "Hello Boys" written in large, bold text, she wears only a lacy black pushup bra and matching panties, flaunting her perfectly buxom breasts. Compared with these women, I never made the cut. I felt like I needed to possess their body shape to be beautiful.

If I saw far more examples of beautiful women with smaller breasts also celebrated, would I have undergone the transformation?

I might have been brainwashed by the lush blond women bouncing toward me on my television screen, but there's no denying that the surgery ratcheted my confidence sky-high. Just months after recovering, I started pursuing pinup modeling aggressively. I was no longer scared of the movement of a boyfriend's hand toward my breasts, now excited to unveil them, anticipating that grateful, dumbstruck expression on men's faces when they see a woman's nakedness for the first time.

My new breasts made me feel like an equal rival to Cherise. Initially, her presence on campus made me feel inferior and interchangeable. In my mind we were pitted as competition against each other. My deep insecurities meant that I needed to be unique, and the experience of having a "twin" amplified my fears of disappearing faceless into a harem of silky hair, diminutive statures, and foxy eyes. The first day of sophomore year, with my new breasts, I walked onto campus feeling emboldened. But I hardly saw Cherise around campus that year and have no idea what happened to her after college. She's not on social media. All I know is what my classmate told me—that she married one of the Chinese frat guys from Lambda Phi Epsilon.

I wonder if she was ever approached by strangers stopping her on the street and calling her Kayla Yu (probably mispronouncing my stage name as everyone did, after I became infamous online).

CHINA DOLLS

My longest relationship as a young adult was with Don, who was instrumental in boosting my confidence to pursue modeling. He was Korean American, six foot three and slim, with a zero fade, and he frequently wore wife beaters, basketball shorts, and brightly colored Nike Dunks.

I was attracted to Korean men long before K-pop became mainstream and BTS topped the charts and covers of American magazines. They had height, square jaws, and sharply defined features and entranced me with their domineering ways. My friends and I joked that Korean men were "wife beaters" because they had a reputation for domestic abuse. This did not deter my desire; in fact, it fueled it. I saw it as a mutinous act against my domineering tiger mom, as if gravitating toward controlling alpha men would prevent me from becoming her. There were scant numbers of Asian women in the media during the mid-1990s, and the few gracing our television screens in the early 2000s were mostly dragon ladies or wilting creatures devoted to pleasing men. The thick vein of these tropes swelled underneath the background of American culture, and I acted accordingly. Because I didn't want to be like my mother—overbearing and controlling—I preferred to be the embodiment of desirable sweetness, a delicate flower twisting up toward my man as if he were the sun. Throughout my relationship with Don and in later ones, I associated submissiveness with being the perfect girlfriend.

Don was a friend of my UCSD crew, and we'd encounter each other when he visited my friends in our freshman dorms. When we made eye contact, dormant sparks crackled to life inside. We hardly spoke, but I learned from friends that he thought I was hot. One weekend, my college friends and I drove up to Cerritos in southeastern Los Angeles (one of California's cities with a majority Asian demographic currently) for Don's birthday house party. His parents were out of town, and when we arrived, drunk young men and the smoky stink of weed filled his family home. Don was nowhere to be found. Tupac's *Greatest Hits* boomed over cheap speakers as we drank budget soju from red Solo cups while smoking Marlboro Reds. After thirty minutes, he emerged from his bedroom and bounded down the stairs.

"Oh, hey, beautiful," he said. His attention electrified me. I reveled in male attention; if there wasn't a man I fancied shooting his masculinity in my direction, I was uninspired. He grinned widely at our guy friends, exchanging telepathic secrets through the air, the details floating entirely above my head. I later learned he had a girl nicknamed Kitten upstairs. His friends delivered her as some kind of sexual gift, although I never saw her that night—she was like a filmy tissue he crumpled and discarded after use. "How are you?" he asked me after high-fiving his friends.

"Super sleepy," I said truthfully, exhausted after our long drive up.

"You can sleep in my parents' bed!" he said, ceremoniously thrusting the doors open to reveal the king-size bed in the master bedroom. "It's all yours." He grinned.

I slept peacefully through the night, and he didn't sneak in, although part of me hoped he would. The following day, he took me to breakfast, and I found myself in another instant relationship. In the following weeks, we spent hours together on the phone.

He flattered me, calling me his "classy queen" and effortlessly bringing me under his spell. For the first time, I found myself lavished with expensive gifts from a boyfriend. He showered me with pieces from his favorite brand, Moschino, including a black velvet jacket, a shiny formfitting purple minidress, and a monogrammed yellow shirt. I loved the feeling of his lanky, long arms enveloping me, the heat radiating from his chest. Don and his family weren't rich, and I didn't question how a nineteen-year-old afforded such expensive gifts.

"You're superhot because you're elegant. You got class," he told me as I preened, decorated in his gifts and baubles. Accordingly, I developed a taste for Chanel, Prada, Louis Vuitton, and Moschino. I didn't notice how quickly it clicked into my new normal.

Don flooded me with so many compliments and presents that

I never noticed the negging.* Negging is a practice that was popularized by pickup artists on the 2007 VH1 show *The Pickup Artist* and *The New York Times* bestselling book *Rules of the Game* by Neil Strauss. It's a form of manipulation where the man deliberately insults or gives backhanded compliments to a woman to diminish her self-confidence and make her more receptive to sexual and emotional control. I doubt Don did it consciously, but I already suffered from low self-esteem, so it affected me quite a bit.

One time, while driving in his dad's black Nissan Pathfinder, as he rapped along to Tupac's "California Love," he suddenly blurted out, "Girls with short hair are so hot." I immediately felt self-conscious about my cherished long hair cascading to the middle of my back. Soon after, I trimmed my hair half a foot to just above my shoulders, splitting the difference as I didn't have the face or beauty to pull off anything shorter. I was sad to see my long locks hit the floor, but pleasing him was superior to my desires.

Besides altering my looks, I appeased him in other ways, striving to become the perfect girlfriend. He was a daily pot smoker, never far from his three-foot glass bong. He often pushed it toward me. I found the idea of sucking at the open end of a glass pipe and inhaling a lungful of smoke—held as long as possible—repulsive. The puff of air exhaled smelled putrid. But I eventually caved to please him. It was awful, and he was a terrible weed

---

* Although flawed, Don was far from a villain. We were a pair of dumb teenagers when we first started dating, and I was hardly the perfect girlfriend. To his credit, he was incredibly supportive of my modeling aspirations and complimented me endlessly about my looks.

partner. Instead of ensuring I felt safe and secure, he hated that weed didn't give me the heady, relaxed feeling he enjoyed. I felt bouts of terrible, peaky paranoia, becoming hyperaware of my senses in an anxiety-inducing way. Each breath, swallow, and blink bred a low-level panic. After that first time, I told Don I didn't want to smoke anymore, but he'd push the bong toward me again and again. I submitted to make him happy. He also later introduced me to ecstasy and raves.

—

Submissiveness is a trait rooted in Asian patriarchy, and in retrospect, it probably had a major influence on how I behaved in relationships. The first time I became aware of Asian culture's inherent misogyny was in junior high after my aunt handed me *The Joy Luck Club* by Amy Tan. Her 1989 novel was groundbreaking; after its success, publishers were much more willing to work with first-time Asian American authors. The 1993 movie adaptation of the book was also a huge success and a major milestone for Asian American culture as one of the first films with Asian American representation, and it grossed a healthy $32.9 million. Sadly, it would still be twenty-five years until another Asian American–centered studio film, *Crazy Rich Asians,* graced the silver screen.

I loved reading and voraciously whipped through the book in one weekend. I'd never come across a book about Chinese Americans and felt like it was written for me, even as a Taiwanese American. *The Joy Luck Club* tells the story of four Chinese American daughters and their relationships and conflicts with their immigrant mothers. It artfully weaves together multiple complicated storylines and themes of generational trauma, illustrating the richness and complexity of Chinese heritage. As I read the book, the mothers' stories resonated more than the daughters'. The mothers' collective hardship in China haunted me, making me feel grateful I was raised in the United States. They suffered terrible ordeals under the Chinese patriarchy, losing children, being separated from families, and marrying terrible men. Women in China were expected to exhibit qualities of obedience and compliant subordination. They didn't dare fantasize about their own dreams; they were expected to treat men as gods and to bear sons. Although the daughters triumph over adversity by the book's conclusion, most of the characters—both mothers and daughters—spend much of the narrative in submission.

The movie in particular is clearly designed for Western audiences, framed as an educational look at a foreign land. The mothers, growing up in China, are deferential and compliant because, under Confucianism, women had to follow the Three Obediences, Four Virtues, and Seven Grounds. The Three Obediences stated that Chinese women first had to obey their fathers, then husbands, and finally sons. The Four Virtues laid out a code of conduct. The Seven Grounds were the bases for divorce, including not bearing a son, talking too much, or having an incurable disease. There is a cultural element to patriarchal practices in Asian countries, and one could argue producers were just following the storyline in the book (Tan herself was one of the producers), but I do believe that they could have made artistic choices in the score, costume, and set design that empowered the characters without reducing them to caricatures. Throughout, China is exoticized and othered in flashbacks layered with leisurely erhu-tinged Chinese music. Chinese proverbs are quoted by the mothers, who speak in broken English, which makes them seem particularly "other." In more recent years, *The Joy Luck Club* has been criticized for perpetuating stereotypes, despite being a groundbreaking work, and combined with the more racial aesthetics in the film, it did contribute to Western society's narrative and perception, in the 1990s and 2000s, that Asian women were foreign, docile, submissive, and easily taken advantage of.

—

In my parents' household, even though we lived in America, the Asian subordination of women still flew across oceans, weaving its influence on my family. My mother taught me to respect and defer to authority figures, especially men. Her father, whom we called Ah Gong, was a stoic figure. I don't remember saying more than a few words to him, but all the women in my family catered to him. And although he spoke rarely, if Ah Gong gave a command, everyone obeyed without question. At the time, I just understood it as being respectful of your elders, a key Confucian principle.

My mother and her sister moved to the United States because, as women, they would not inherit the family's very successful industrial business. My mom was the oldest of four, but as a daughter, ownership passed to her two younger brothers. She dreamed of becoming a lawyer but gave that up, too, following my father to Lawrence, Kansas, where he had an engineering scholarship at the University of Kansas. Instead, she became a homemaker until she went to work after I started elementary school.

When I got older, she confided to me that she had waited on my father hand and foot, while he never lifted a finger in the household. As a child, I didn't notice because it appeared as if she ruled with an iron fist. She was terrifying, and I presumed she was in charge. But the patriarchal underpinnings were right under my nose. My mother cooked, cleaned, disciplined, and raised my brother and me on top of working a full-time job. My gentle dad was unwittingly the quintessential Asian patriarch. Although not domineering, he naturally assumed what he'd learned in Taiwanese culture: solely women handled the housework and child-rearing. He went to work, came home, and kicked his feet up, watching *Married . . . with Children* on TV and treating my mother as his maid and cook. I never connected the dots between my mother dutifully managing the house and the patriarchy and subordination until I was older.

Just like the daughters in *The Joy Luck Club*, I had no understanding of the hopes and dreams my mother carried with her when she immigrated to America. The movie portrayed a far more nuanced and accurate representation of the experiences of Asian women past and present compared with other existing media at the time. But it still portrayed submissive Asian women twisting and bending backward for their husbands.

Of all the daughters in the movie, Lena annoyed me the most. She seemed spineless, becoming diminished in a marital facade of "fairness." She marries her boss, an older Chinese American man making seven times her income, who forces her to pay 50 percent of all household expenses, except for personal items like shaving cream and tampons. Even after gifting her a cat, he splits the full cost of the cat's flea medicine. When she finally confronts him, furious about paying 50 percent for ice cream she never eats, he negs her: "I thought you were dieting." He defends this absurdity as fairness and equality and suggests she rethink their marriage entirely. It isn't a conversation; it is a silencing. She has no room to defend herself; he mansplains until he abruptly ends the conversation.

Lena's passivity is illuminated by her mother, Ying-ying. In a vulnerable moment, Ying-ying admits her daughter had no self-worth or spirit because she had none to give. We learn that Lena isn't Ying-ying's first child—there was an earlier husband and family. Back in China, Ying-ying married a handsome, chivalrous, and charming man named Lin Xiao, and their sexual chemistry was off the charts. But after Ying-ying bore his son, Lin Xiao flagrantly cheated on her with a beautiful opera singer, and Ying-ying was relegated to nanny and maid in her own home. After becoming a mother, her worth as a woman was gone in his eyes. He moved on to his next conquest, reducing her to his house servant. Consumed by powerlessness, Ying-ying did the unforgivable: she drowned her baby son in a futile attempt at revenge, a desperate grab for control when she had none.

Both women feel helpless under their husband's rule, even though one grew up in China and the other was born and raised in America. Despite the vast cultural and generational divide, both Ying-ying's cruel Chinese husband and Lena's petty Chinese American husband expect their wife's self-sacrifice. Whether an accurate portrayal of the Asian patriarchy or not, the movie and book convey a troubling message to Western viewers that Asian women are easily silenced and sidelined. This is even more concerning when we realize schools require malleable young kids to read the book as a cultural study. *The Joy Luck Club* is a stellar work of art, and it should be taught in schools, but only properly. Teachers cannot lead with Confucian values of submissiveness, because once non-Asian men start yearning for this subservient stereotype, it takes on an unmistakably sexual tinge.

Asiaphiles often say they prefer Asian women for their superior family values. When I posted a video on TikTok about yellow fever, one viewer wrote, "Asian women typically value family, are skinny. . . . That's why we like them. Not the weird submissive shit." I'm not sure he realized what Asiaphiles often mean when praising Asian women as "good wives with family values." It's a belief rooted in romanticized views of cultural differences, specifically that Asian women fulfill patriarchal ideals. "Family oriented," in the Asiaphile's fantasy of Asian women, implies sacrifice, obedience, and an assumption that the wife does exactly as she's told—sometimes including degrading sex—without asking for anything in return. The belief is that she elevates her family's and husband's needs before her own. We often forget that it's an ideology rooted in misogyny, anti-feminism, and colonialism.

We forget that thousands of Japanese women left Japan after World War II, marrying American servicemen during America's occupation of the defeated country. Following the passage of the 1945 War Brides Act, as many as forty-five thousand Japanese women emigrated from cities like Tokyo to the United States to reunite with American husbands in states such as Delaware, Kansas, and Rhode Island. According to the Smithsonian, it was by far the largest female-only immigration circumstance in U.S. history and increased the Asian American population by 10 percent. These women were pressured to assimilate to their new country.

The Red Cross in Japan opened bride schools, which taught Japanese women how to be docile and obedient wives. Education included cooking American foods, performing household chores, applying makeup, and walking in high heels. These women are the origins upon which the Asian American model minority myth was built. From 1947 to 1964, at least 72,700 Asian women immigrated to the States from Japan, the Philippines, Korea, and China, according to the U.S. Immigration and Naturalization Service. This is considered a highly conservative estimate; some put the figure to be more likely around 150,000. At the same time, according to Celine Parreñas Shimizu in *The Hypersexuality of Race*, pornography highlighting sexually and domestically servile Asian women as the ideal partners for American men also became popular. This is what Asiaphiles mean when they celebrate "family-oriented" Asian women under the guise of cultural admiration.

Confucian principles may be at play, but many Asian women left their homelands to escape those dated teachings. My mother and the mothers in *The Joy Luck Club* were among this demographic, yet they couldn't escape the Asian patriarchy. As my mother's daughter, I watched and I learned from her actions. She never explicitly told me to bend to my boyfriends' whims, but still, I inherited her deference to men, emulating it in my most significant relationships and my career—even if subconsciously.

It all started with Don. After Don and I broke up years later, I was never quite as submissive in relationships as I was with him, but I still spent the next decade of my career reenacting the narratives dictated to me by the Asian and Western patriarchy. Their influence on me is evident. I ended up as digital chattel for the whimsies and sexual fantasies of Asiaphiles. I considered myself different from the women of *The Joy Luck Club* and my mother—all-American and not under the thumb of the restrictive Asian patriarchy—but I did worse. I showcased my deference and objectified myself as a pinup model, feeding into the Western fantasy of the Orient that Asian women existed to serve men.

BAD ASIAN

"Give me one of your cigarettes!" I demanded of my friend Alan one weekend.

The first time I smoked a cigarette was freshman year of college. Attending UCSD was my first taste of freedom, and away from my tiger mom's watchful eye I could rebel without consequences. I thought UCSD would be a party school because it was just a fifteen-minute drive from San Diego State University (SDSU), which was one of America's most famously wild schools and deemed as such for four consecutive years by *Playboy* magazine. Although we looked down at SDSU for its lower academics, its campus was far more exciting. UCSD was boring in comparison, the campus sitting in the quiet retirement community of La Jolla. During weekends, we could only cruise the city, watch TV, or try to sneak into an SDSU party.

"Have you even tried a cigarette before?" Alan replied.

I shook my head no.

"These are Reds." He motioned to his box of Marlboros. "They'll kill you. Let's grab you something lighter."

Alan thought I was making a spur-of-the-moment decision, but I had wanted to start smoking for a while. In high school, there were the cool Asians with their lowered Japanese cars and the nerdy ones, and I'd been a cross of both. Mainly because of my mom's steely gaze, I fit into the mold of the model minority myth, an assumption that Asians are quiet, intelligent, high achieving, and hardworking. This stereotype was invented by white supremacists to pit Asians against other minorities. Their logic was "If Asians had no problem scaling economic, social, and academic ladders, why couldn't other ethnic groups do the same?"

In popular media, Asians were either nerds or highly sexualized. One enduring example of the nerdy Asian is Takashi from *Revenge of the Nerds*, which premiered in 1984 and had three sequels, with the last in 1994. Played by Brian Tochi, Takashi has a thick Japanese accent. He's a geeky, polite, and deferential Asian man constantly tricked by white frat boys. In college, I wanted absolutely no connection with that embarrassing stereotype, and an easy way to rebel was to pick up a cigarette. Smoking is starting to become rare, but in the late nineties, it was ubiquitous, at least with the edgy Asians at my school.

Alan took me to a gas station, and I perused the dizzying array of multicolored cigarette boxes on display.

"Have you heard of Benson and Hedges?" he asked.

I shook my head.

"I think you'll like it. It's a good starter cigarette; girls love them."

Benson and Hedges 100s are longer and thinner than the average cigarette and primarily marketed at women. The golden cardboard box, which appeared much more expensive and elegant than the plain Marlboro one, seemed an effortless gateway to cool. The thin layer of plastic wrap was easily peeled off by my acrylic French manicured nails. I imagined myself as a glamorous Parisian, smoking while waving away a plate of food, saying, "Oh no, I'm not hungry; I'll have a cigarette instead." As the cigarette met my lips, I felt a slight heady buzz, but it was as light as smoking air. Smoking back then, for me, was all for show.

A week later, I purchased a shiny gold Zippo lighter, fully committing to my new habit. I loved clicking it open and flicking the jagged wheel to spark a flame. Smoking was more ritual than physical addiction. I loved a cigarette in hand for all occasions, and it quickly became routine. Soon I anticipated the morning cigarette, the after-meal one; smoking with friends after class, while driving; and any other occasion I could use as an excuse to grab a smoke. By the time I was a sophomore, I'd graduated to smoking much stronger Marlboro menthols to impress Don, who smoked Reds. Don paid me many compliments, but the underlying feeling of being nerdy, ugly, and defective—of being a dog—never entirely left me.

Yet Don's frequent praise built my confidence. "You should model; you're just as pretty as the Asian pinup girls," he'd tell me. In retrospect, he was a bit of a flatterer and probably said the same to all his exes, but I lapped it up like a starving kitten and decided to actively pursue modeling. Despite fantasizing in high school about becoming like Sung-Hi Lee one day, I hadn't yet attempted to break into the industry. Don's comments were an encouraging reminder and the push I needed to take the leap. That it made my boyfriend happy was a bonus.

The only problem was I had zero knowledge of how to start, and there was no one to ask. La Jolla was a wholesome, affluent seaside community—hardly the hotbed of pinup modeling. The internet was still in its infancy, so I looked through school paper ads and local newspapers, submitting photos to castings blindly—a fatal mistake. There were several sizable universities in the area, and college co-eds away from home for the first time were prime targets for predators. I was blissfully unaware of the proliferation of sharks hunting vulnerable young women aspiring to model in San Diego.* Because of yellow fever, I was also at higher risk. But I was completely naive. I had a vague sense of the Asian fetish at the time, but it wasn't something I encountered in real life. Unknowingly, yellow fever combined with desperation to break into modeling would lead me straight into a predator's den.

One of my first photo shoots was with a random middle-aged white guy in the bright and airy kitchen of his very average house in the San Diego suburbs. Another Asian model was on her way out as I entered.

"This is one of the calendars I produce," he said proudly, handing it to me to flip through as I sat across from him at his kitchen table.

---

* I wasn't the only victim. Years later, in 2020, twenty-two victims won a civil case against GirlsDoPorn, a pornographic website operating out of San Diego from 2009 to 2020. The six men involved were charged with sex trafficking by coercion, force, and fraud.

I wasn't impressed. It was low caliber with lousy lighting and cheap paper. The Asian models filling its pages were far from the stunning glamazons featured in the high-end glossies Sung-Hi modeled for. But I didn't want to be rude and was eager to start modeling, so I smiled tightly and said, "It looks great."

"Are you ready to shoot some photos?" he asked. "I've got a box of clothing you can use." He motioned to a box of cloth scraps that barely qualified as clothing, nothing I would actually wear, but it didn't matter; it wasn't a fashion shoot. All I had were a couple of poorly shot photos taken by my boyfriend in my dorm room. I needed to build my portfolio.

Since high school, I'd studied the models in Victoria's Secret catalogs and *Sports Illustrated* swimsuit issues and memorized Sung-Hi's best stances. I was eager to show off my slinky posing techniques. I stretched my limbs and curved my spine suggestively for the camera as he exclaimed, "That's gorgeous, hold that," and "Beautiful, you're perfect," and "You were born for this." Photographers say these things to all models to make them more comfortable and confident, but it never failed to boost my ego.

"Before you leave, I want to show you something," the photographer said, as the shoot came to a close. He motioned to his computer, asking his assistant to pull up a web page filled with a dizzying array of pixelated and thumbnailed Asian women performing hardcore sex acts. "You're a natural model, but I also produce these videos. You can make so much more money as an adult performer."

"I'm not interested in that at all," I told him with a tight laugh, collecting my stuff and leaving his house in a petulant huff. I was above *that* type of modeling.

A week later, he contacted me again. "The photos turned out fantastic. Let me know if you ever want to shoot again and if you wanna take your career to the next level as an adult performer!"

Ew, I thought. I already told him I wasn't interested, and my mind wouldn't change just a week or so later.

Men like him were constantly trying to push me into hardcore porn. At another "audition," the white "casting director," after finding out that I was a massive fan of Sung-Hi's, said, "It's a little-known fact that Sung-Hi launched her career starring in hardcore porn videos. She wore a wig and looked completely different, but if you look closely, you can tell it's her."

He could be telling the truth, I thought naively. This was before everything was available on the internet and when VHS tapes were still the primary outlet for porn distribution, so there was no easy way to verify his claim unless I happened upon the same tape. But even if he wasn't just fabricating information to persuade me, I was vehemently against it. Yes, I wanted to be as adored as Sung-Hi and was ready to bend some rules, but hardcore pornography was not one of them. To youthful me, it seemed the ultimate stigma of whoredom. As a nineteen-year-old virgin with only some over-the-clothes heavy-petting sessions with my boyfriend, there was no way I'd perform my first sexual acts on camera.

But despite having zero intention of becoming a pornographic performer, I still found myself caught in the web of a practiced predator finessed at tricking, coercing, and assaulting women into performing sexual acts on camera. The next ad I got a response from was a casting call for swimsuit and pinup models. Because the ad appeared in the UCSD school newspaper, it lulled me into a false sense of safety, and I didn't expect any danger lurking behind it. I'm appalled the "casting director" was able to post in the school paper, but there was likely no screening process for the "want ads" section, meaning anyone could place one. He was another middle-aged man sitting behind a small office desk in a strip mall. He looked like your average white dude, nondescript, with dark brown hair.

"You've got a great look," he said. "I could definitely get you in these magazines and calendars." He handed me a stack of glossy publications with gorgeous models and high-end photography.

As the trusting ingenue, I took his promise at face value and left hopeful, with a test shoot scheduled days later. That test shoot was in his dingy apartment lair, which looked exactly like the setting of an amateur porno. Other sketchy castings I went to were in homes, so it didn't seem odd to me this shoot took place at his apartment. But the moment I stepped in, I sensed something was off—a subtle shift in the atmosphere, so slight it could easily be dismissed. Unbeknownst to me, I had walked onto a gonzo-style porn set.

Gonzo porn—a moniker dripping with raunch—is a cheap and easy-to-film style of pornography featuring first-person-style shooting. Because of its ease to film, it was steadily gaining popularity at the time and killed the market for "high-end" pornography produced by studios such as Vivid Entertainment and Wicked Pictures and featuring superstars like Jenna Jameson, Asia Carrera, and Kobe Tai. Usually, the man filming the scene with a handheld camera was also the performer.

In my video, the premise was the generic porn trope of "man lures woman into his apartment with the promise of a casting but instead coerces sex acts." Three other women, all Asian, also appear with the videographer/assailant in the video; I assume the premise was the same for them. According to the VHS box cover, we're all nineteen or twenty years old—sexual roadkill, barely of age, revving up Asian fetishists with yellow fever.

Ultimately, we were just casualties of the sleek and insidious patriarchal machinery of pornography, where "Asian" is one of the most popular categories. Porn superstar Asa Akira mentioned in her memoir that there's always a shortage of Asian performers, never enough to meet demand. This doesn't mean that there is a lack of representation of Asian women in porn, but rather that the demand for porn featuring Asian women is so high, there aren't enough actresses to churn out sufficient content. In 2011, *Complex* magazine published "The Top 50 Hottest Asian Porn Stars of All Time." It would be difficult, if not impossible, to compile a list of the top fifty Asian American female actresses or singers back then. In "Gender, Race, and Aggression in Mainstream Pornography," the sociologists Eran Shor and Golshan Golriz conclude that "the pornography industry is one of the few media where Latina and Asian women have relatively higher visibility and points to the possible importance of this industry in shaping and reproducing stereotypes about women from these groups."

The most searched terms on Pornhub in 2022 include "hentai" (anime porn) at number one and "Japanese" at number two. These first two searches have a massive lead on the remaining key words, although "Pinay" appears at number five and "Asian"—the catchall—at number six. Out of thirty search terms, only four other ethnic search terms were included: "Latina" at number eleven, "ebony" at number twelve, "Indian" at number twenty-four, and "Black" at number twenty-six. The irony is that despite the popularity of Asian porn, only one Asian porn star appeared on the list "Most Searched for Porn Stars" on Pornhub: Rae Lil Black, at number twenty-one of thirty. For the list "Most Viewed Amateur Models," there were two Asian performers out of thirty, Luna Okko at number nineteen and Obokozu at number twenty-seven. The fact that the most popular search terms on Pornhub are Asian but the most popular names for porn stars and amateur models are not Asian suggests that fans of Asian-related porn view Asian women as nameless and interchangeable toys. It shows that the identity of the Asian woman doesn't matter, only that she be Asian.

There is little imagination to the most common themes in Asian porn, nothing else to the storyline other than the performer is Asian. According to Shimizu, the categories included "girls from the Orient, young girls (uniformed schoolgirls or poor enslaved girls forced to sell their bodies), the fetishized racial difference in interracial sex, spoils of war, prostitutes, anal sex, and the discourse of stereotypes such as the model minority, the good student, and the small servile body as a pre-feminist haven." In other words, in Asian pornography the category is highly racialized and inextricable from colonialism and domination. Unlike other generic porn tropes, where the race of the woman doesn't matter—pizza delivery, cable outage, lifeguard at the beach—the story in Asian porn is intrinsically tied to ethnicity. Violence is also a common refrain in porn featuring Asian women. These harmful beliefs fueled some of the most disturbing comments on my later fan site. My manager's assistant who ran my Yahoo page recalls multiple daily comments that described raping me, beating and strangling me, slapping me, making me bleed, kicking me, stomping on me, and other acts of aggression. If the comments weren't about rape, they were about inflicting pain in a variety of ways. A common topic was having anal sex with me and wanting to fuck me until I cried or split in half. The constant refrain was degrading me in some way, everything from having me crawl and beg for sex to forcing me to eat dog food. The men on my fan site would describe their cum in every conceivable way—making me eat it or releasing it on my face, feet, and every other body part. One man wanted me to drink it out of a baby bottle, and another said that he'd let me eat it with chopsticks. One comment my manager's assistant says she'll never forget is one man saying he wanted to get me pregnant so he could abort the baby. Many of these violent images are perpetuated in porn, and it's not surprising that these ideas can eventually lead to violence and that some men will attempt to act out these ideas in real life.

Porn featuring Asian women is almost always degrading and often violent, but it's important to note that some famous Asian porn stars have spoken out about their consensual performances as an act of feminism. Annabel Chong is one example. In her film *The World's Biggest Gang Bang*, for over ten hours, 251 men penetrated her, breaking the record for participants and pumping and thrusting the hypersexual Asian trope into the digisphere. Media coverage proliferated into even mainstream outlets.

When she was asked why she shot the porn, she said, "I hate going on dates, but I still want to get laid," and that having sex with 251 guys for ten hours was no different from having sex with one guy for ten hours. Chong argued she was making a feminist statement with acts of whoredom against the limitations of the Asian fetish and flouting the model minority myth, which she represented as a University of Southern California student, but one could argue that she instead gave the hypersexual Asian stereotype vertebrae to prop up its spine. Chong paraded that stereotype on talk shows like *The Jerry Springer Show* and discussed it in an equally disturbing documentary about her life, which screened at Sundance and was nominated for a Sundance Grand Jury Prize.

In *Sex: The Annabel Chong Story*, Chong reveals she was gang-raped by six men while attending college in London. She revisits the rape site while the voice-over explains she thought these men might kill her, so she allowed it mechanically until it was over. It's possible she was making a feminist statement by taking ownership of her victimization through reenacting an extreme version of the rape with 251 men, and perhaps it returned some agency both to her and to other Asian women who have felt degraded by the porn industry, but Chong's graphic display of self-harm in her documentary, slicing into her arm expertly and viciously with a knife, begs the question of how effective this experiment was for her mental health.

I cannot speak for Chong or other Asian porn stars, but at least for me, reframing participation in a porn as a feminist act does little to alleviate the trauma of being sexualized, used, and trafficked for male pleasure. Even when porn or public nudity is consensual and violence-free, it fuels the patriarchal fantasy of the hypersexual or submissive Asian woman. Amy Sun perfectly encapsulates it in her essay "Mainstream Porn Has Taught You a Lot About Asian Female Sexuality—But It's All a Direct Result of Racism," writing, "Asian women are the model minority—*even in porn*. We are lithe, tight, and ready to go with a smile."

———

For my part, I remember very little of that day except for a few disturbing flashes of imagery I'd rather forget. I can't explain what happened, but I'm unequivocally certain that if my assailant had asked me to shoot a pornographic video, I would have said no, as I'd already said to several pornographers before him. I must have been in shock and subsequently shut down and dissociated—blacked out.

There I was, alone in that room with a much older and larger white man who had lured me to his apartment under false pretenses. I weighed barely a hundred pounds and wore little clothing. No one in the world knew where I was. He could hurt or even kill me, and no one would know. At that moment, my young mind likely decided it best to be completely compliant. It's a known trauma and threat response, one of fight, flight, freeze, or fawn. Fawn means you please or placate your assailant to protect yourself, especially if they are bigger and stronger and there's a power imbalance. I did as he commanded. He asked to penetrate me, then tried for a blow job, but I said I couldn't comply because I had never performed either act before. By the time I left the videotaped "test shoot," he'd coerced me into performing several other explicit sex acts for the first time. They were not consensual.

While researching this book, I watched the video for the first time in its entirety since I shot it more than twenty-five years ago. Not wanting to fully relive the experience, I mostly fast-forwarded through, needing to get a sense of what millions saw. I'm horrified by the parts he included. There were fake smiles at the beginning, footage shot before I realized what would transpire. Later, as I was trapped and unable to say no, I mostly stared into space with confusion and evident discomfort. That disorientation soon morphs into visible flashes of fear. My guess is that he left those parts in purposefully for a very specific class of men who would enjoy my distress. Much of the video is also out of sequence to appear like I continue to smile at the end of the video, after I've been assaulted.

Watching it back, I wanted to roar at my teenage self, "Get the fuck out, RUN!" But would my timid and obedient self *really* have torn out of the room naked into the apartment complex? Unlikely. At that age, level of naivete, and lack of experience, once wheels were in motion, I had no idea how to stop things until they ran their course.

Yet, "Why didn't you just leave?" is the same question I've asked myself countless times. That thought and the video have haunted me for more than twenty-five years. What hurt most in the aftermath was the reaction of people close to me, who saw me not as a victim but as a willing volunteer. Years later, a boyfriend said, "I don't judge you for anything you've done in the past, but I know that you've performed sexual acts for money." Things went sideways when I tried to explain that I hadn't done so willingly. He simply couldn't understand how I could be a victim if no physical force—a knife or a gun—was involved. "It's not like you were raped," he said. What he failed to understand was that sexual violence doesn't always entail physical force; perpetrators of sexual violence may also use psychological force or manipulation to coerce a victim into nonconsensual sex acts. No matter what I said, he couldn't understand I was a teenager who was assaulted and trafficked.

———

After the shoot, I fully dissociated. I have no recollection of driving home or getting home, if I went to school the next day, what I said to my boyfriend. I never told him about the incident. In a hazy memory, more like a dream and probably my imagination, I see myself showering, then taking a scalding bath and submerging my head underwater to scream.

The memory was jettisoned so far down I never thought of it again until the video later released. I didn't tell a soul and continued to attend my classes and local parties. In the early 2000s, rave culture became a dominant American subculture that took over the Asian American community. Although raves were mostly white, their messaging was inclusive under the acronym PLUR: peace, love, unity, and respect. Droves of Asian Americans attended, rebelling against the model minority myth by ingesting massive amounts of drugs. At raves, we could wear our ethnicity like a loose garment instead of restrictive armor. Not long before shooting the video, Don had taken me to a rave. My first rave found me crumpled to the filthy ground of the Glass House in Pomona, California, with a pacifier in my mouth and a Pikachu backpack slipping off my shoulders. I was instantly hooked, and in the aftermath of my assault, what was at first a wonderful escape from the stress of classes and exams eventually became an obliteration of all my senses and everything I wanted to forget.

Raves were an egalitarian utopia where our past poor decisions and race didn't matter. They were the perfect escape from my recent trauma.

I sank deeper into bliss.

On ecstasy, a green triangle Don placed on my tongue like a Communion wafer, every part of my body tingled to the booming bass beat of techno as undulating joy tidal-waved over me. I felt pure love for everyone, but especially me. I accepted myself as perfect and whole, with nothing to prove. The world smiled like clouds of cotton candy. No longer feeling of solid form, my every cell and atom seemed to vibrate at a higher frequency. The release was like the relief of warm conditioner in the shower slicing through gnarled tangled hair. I was fluid and transient, yet infinite. It was unbelievable that such a feeling existed, and my introversion dissipated as I welcomed strangers swiping thick layers of Vicks VapoRub under my nose and performing impromptu frenzied glow stick dances inches from my face. Sadly, that holy feeling never lasted longer than my high.

Cigarettes and Don became my constant rave companions. I graduated to Newports, one of the strongest menthol cigarettes with some of the highest nicotine levels on the market. It was rumored menthol cigarettes contained fiberglass, making them more damaging than other cigarettes (proven untrue), but I didn't give a shit. We menthol smokers purchased Ice Drops breath freshener from the gas station and squeezed a drop or two onto the unlit end to give the cigarette a supercharged minty zing. It seemed to enhance my high every time I inhaled. I chain-smoked all night, finding escape and forgetting about desperately needing beauty and validation. On drugs, my assault never happened, and I wasn't damaged goods. Every night I felt young and wild and full of thousands of possibilities.

I had never felt such peace, so I let myself fall.

Spiraling into heavy drug use, I no longer cared what went in my body, trying any substance handed to me. I felt like trash when my high wore off and constantly sought out anything that could give me a buzz. I wasn't consciously trying to escape the video; I just couldn't handle being on campus anymore. In the aftermath, there was little I could stomach; I was a walking frayed and exposed nerve ending. Though I shoved the memory miles past consciousness, forgetting it happened, that level of disassociation left me disconnected from everything and everyone around me. Being around my classmates felt exhausting. My body no longer felt like my own. The only time I felt anything was from a cigarette's buzzy menthol kick or the happy obliteration of ecstasy. The drug-filled reverie and disassociation may have been my body's subconscious way of protecting itself.

My GPA dropped to 2.5. The only grace was that it helped convince my mom to let me drop out of school—a blessing in disguise. The horror of walking campus halls would have been unimaginable if the video had been released while I was still in school.

———

The drug abuse continued after quitting UCSD. Months later, I enrolled at Rio Hondo College, a community college in Whittier, California. Unlike at UCSD, where I dormed on campus for two years and had a tight-knit circle of friends, I was anonymous. I kept my head down, took classes, and didn't speak to anyone. Between classes, I lived at my friend Sara's house in Chino Hills with my boyfriend Don. Lost in a trance of ecstasy-soaked rave haze, I camped out in her upstairs bedroom on a mattress on the floor. The place was filthy; her dog defecated all over the living room, and no one cleaned it. But I was slowly starting to get my act back together. I started to build up my modeling portfolio, forgetting earlier failed attempts had led me into danger.

One of my first pinup photographers was Julie Strain. She was the go-to for Playmates and pinups such as Dita Von Teese, Devin DeVasquez, Shae Marks, and many more. Julie was talented at her craft, teaching a fine art and photography class at UCLA and shooting for pinup print magazines. As a self-made woman, Julie also empathized with aspiring pinups like me. She'd slowly climbed from the bottom ranks to become *Penthouse* Pet of the Month in 1991 and Pet of the Year in 1993. Using those magazine covers as a platform to catapult her career, she became a cult icon and B-movie megastar. In a short time, she starred in her own comic book, hosted a show on the Playboy Channel, and was the main character in the animated feature film *Heavy Metal 2000*, distributed by Columbia TriStar. "Six foot one and worth the climb!" was her tagline. She had a great sense of humor.

I inquired about a shoot, and she promptly responded with her $500 rate. By this time, I had racked up over $4,000 on my first credit card, which was pushed on college co-eds like me on the UCSD campus during freshman orientation week. Enticed by the complimentary toiletry samples at the Visa booth, my charge card became an instant addiction. I never learned to manage finances and purchased a pair of $500 black platform Prada shoes, along with other pricey items I couldn't afford. What was another $500, charged as a cash advance with exorbitant interest rates? I told myself the photography fee was a career investment.

Shooting with Julie behind the camera was like playing dress-up. Her "playroom" was a glamour girl's dream, an organized jumble of lingerie, bikinis, costumes, and platform heels. For my first look, I chose a bamboo rice hat and blue silk pants printed with Chinese patterns, comfortably leaning into Asian tropes. Topless except for my Asian accessories, that set of photos later appeared on my website under the title "Peasant Girl." The combination of the title, my choice to wear a traditional hat, and the sexualized nudity inadvertently fed straight into the trope of a poor Asian countrywoman hoping to be rescued by a white male savior; it reiterated his destiny to "save" an often decades younger nubile Asian girl from an impoverished country and destitution. It's the premise of the 1955 book *The Quiet American* and its 2002 movie adaptation, where a much older British journalist and a young American soldier battle for the affections of a Vietnamese former taxi dancer named Phuong. They pass her back and forth like a cherished bauble, rationalizing that they're rescuing her from a dire plight in Vietnam. My photos unconsciously sent a similar message of male saviordom. But I wasn't thinking critically about the long-term implications of my actions at this photo shoot. My young mind simply thought, *I'm Asian. Wouldn't Asian accessories look cute on my girlish naked body?*

For the next look, Julie straddled my body, brown curls loose and flowing over her shoulders, clad in cargo pants, a white T-shirt, and Vans sneakers, clasping a DSLR camera in her powerful hands, as I posed on the floor. My body arched on the concrete, naked except for the large swatch of transparent blue Saran wrap clinging to my skin. "You're a sex kitten," she cooed as I contorted my curves while stretching my legs out to the tips of my toes.

After my boob job, I became easily self-confident in my newly curvy body, and I was always comfortable on a professional pinup shoot, considering the photographers had seen countless naked women. My nudity to them was no big deal, I figured. Besides, it was usually a small crew, just the photographer and sometimes a makeup artist and/or videographer. Either way, Julie made me feel exceptionally at ease. She was a true professional, and I enjoyed working with her. It was healing that not everyone in the industry was a slimy man trying to coerce me into hardcore porn. I felt hopeful about the path ahead.

Then, about a year later, I received a call from my UCSD bestie, Stan.

"Is that really you?" he asked. I could hear the pain in his voice over the receiver.

"What are you talking about?" I replied, genuinely confused.

"I saw a disgusting porno video of you. I ran out of the room and threw up."

My heart sank, knowing instantly what he was talking about. "What do you mean?" I asked, panicked.

"Daniel got the video, and we watched it in our dorm room."

I later learned at least six of my guy friends watched the video together. None of these former friends have ever apologized for gathering to watch me, their friend, being assaulted on camera. And none of them ever asked if I was okay after watching it. The traumatic toll of the video never occurred to them.

"When did you shoot it?" he demanded.

"I—I—I don't remember. I guess it was sometime last year," I blurted out, still in shock.

"You shot this while we were friends?" he spat out. "You're disgusting," he said, before hanging up the phone. Our friendship ended there. I ran out of my bedroom and into Sara's room to confide in her.

"He had a knife," I lied as she tried to comfort me. I had no other way of explaining that what was recorded on camera was against my will. I was coerced, yet I knew no one would believe me. It was only years later, when a therapist told me, "That was assault," that another person validated my truth.

My boyfriend entered the bedroom, and I tearfully filled him in on the news. His eyes turned black with fury. Without a word, he left out the front door. Heart dropping, I heard the engine revving on his red Yamaha motorcycle, which I hated. He drove it so recklessly that I refused to ride with him. This time, I thought he was driving out of my life forever. About thirty minutes later he called to say, "I crashed. The bike is totaled." It was a rainy night, and he skidded on the street, fell off, and scratched up his leg, motorcycle slamming into a tree. Luckily no one was hurt, and he escaped with minor injuries. I was happy for the distraction, focusing on taking care of him through the night instead of facing the humiliation of the video. We never discussed the video again, but he stood by me as I dealt with the fallout. I don't know if I could've survived this difficult period without him. My guy friends at UCSD were also his friends, and he never spoke to them again.

Six months later, the video went viral online, and I thought it was the end of my blossoming pinup career. After the negative reaction from friends, I continued modeling and launched my website, shot photos for Sung-Hi's website, and appeared at a few import car shows. But now, with the video gaining popularity, I was forced to confront the emotional trauma, the insufferable shame, self-loathing, and public humiliation. The thought of friends and strangers watching the clip filled me with an existential helplessness. The worst part was everyone thought I performed for money as a willing participant. I confessed about the video to my new webmaster, manager, and agent, thinking they would drop me, but they all continued to support me. My agent, Bill, called my assailant to purchase the video rights. The pornographer replied, "She's blowing the fuck up right now. I'm gonna make a ton off that video, and I'm not selling it back, no matter what."

Bill tried playing to the predator's conscience, saying, "Do you really want to put her in a position that could damage her career moving forward?"

"It's not my problem" was the response. Bill told the pornographer he knew I shot the video against my will, and the pornographer said, "She signed the release."

Ultimately, Bill's legal team advised we had little recourse. This was twenty years before #MeToo, and although I knew I had been assaulted, Bill and I knew many wouldn't understand. When I spoke to Bill years later, he said, "I'll always remember that call because it was the vilest interaction I've ever had in any industry."

———

There's an additional layer of violence when your assault is shared publicly. As horrible as my abuse was, that it existed online was exponentially worse. Each time someone watched a clip from my worst day felt like rape. The enduring perversity of men saving the video of my worst trauma to their computer and copying it to share with friends, replicating it for other pornographic sites, and commemorating my degradation for their unadulterated sexual release was unbearable. To cope, I doubled down on modeling, attempting to scale the heights of online fame, hoping it would erase the scarlet letter on my forehead and fill the gaping wound it gouged inside. Each new magazine cover, photo shoot, and social media follower fused to form a thin shield buttressing me from the utter destruction of people viewing my assault. If I achieved a certain level of success, maybe I would be untouchable and the unconscious psychic pain of my trauma would evaporate.

I also continued to chase the numbing high from drugs. After the initial effervescence passed and things turned dark, I was a periodic, high-functioning addict. I could sober up for a week or two or even a month to prepare for an important photo shoot or musical performance. Still, the moment I was done, I would go on a weeks-long binge or more. I spent years as a vampire, terrified of chirping birds announcing the impending morning light. Too weak to drag myself to the gas station after my cigarettes had run out, I'd sift through the ashtray to smoke unfinished cigarette butts.

When I was finally ready to quit smoking years later, it was even more challenging to kick than my nasty cocaine and pill-popping habit. By then, it was my last major vice. First, I tried a psychic, who "hypnotized" me over the phone. I don't remember what she said and fell asleep halfway through, but I quit smoking for a year. Another time, I attended Nicotine Anonymous meetings, which worked for a bit until I picked up again. Cigarettes were a welcome security blanket in times of stress. Finally, I had my last cigarette after reading Allen Carr's *The Easy Way to Stop Smoking*. Carr tells readers they can continue smoking while reading the 240 pages. I can't explain it, but when I finished reading the book's last page, I never smoked another cigarette again— magically, just as the book promised. It sounds unbelievable, but for me and countless others, the book clicked when nothing else worked. Perhaps it was the combination of everything I had tried to quit smoking coming together after I finished the book. All I know is that for all the years spent smoking and trying to quit, finally ending smoking—that first seemingly teensy rebellion—was a nonevent.

I now see these small rebellions against the model minority myth as an interconnected web of events that led me to my assault. It's the boiling frog metaphor in action. If you throw a frog in boiling water, it'll leap out in a panic. But place it in cool water and slowly raise the heat, and the amphibian remains blissfully unaware, ending up boiled alive. Except in my case, I was both frog and chef. In a revolt against what was expected of me and driven by self-hate, I jumped into the pot, letting myself eventually get boiled alive. Trying that first cigarette felt so innocuous. All the other cool Asians were doing it, so why couldn't I? The problem was that with each small defiance, I felt emboldened to dive further, not realizing the deeper I fell, the harder it would be to emerge unscathed. With each rebellion—smoking, drugs, pinup modeling—I strolled down the path of peril. I was so eager to shed my model minority skin, and so desperate for male validation, that I jumped into opportunities mindlessly, leading me straight into my assailant's trap. If I had paused for even a moment, could things have been different? Or was I too naive and inexperienced to know better? It was that very innocence that made me ripe for his plucking. In hindsight, I could have chosen a path of defiance that didn't deify male regard, but my ferocious hunger for acceptance and depleted self-esteem made me an easy mark. Looking back, I realize how lucky I am that something worse didn't happen.

The video haunted me for years, but when it finally disappeared from the internet, it was as equally anticlimactic as quitting smoking. For more than twenty years, I had tried relentlessly to remove it, emailing website hosts who either ignored me or were hostile. Then suddenly, in December 2020, long after I quit modeling and singing, while the world was in disarray because of a global pandemic, my video was taken down from Pornhub, the world's biggest porn site. This is primarily thanks to Nicholas Kristof's *New York Times* piece "The Children of Pornhub," which accused the company of profiting from videos of exploitation and assault. A week later, Pornhub purged all unverified content— 8.8 million videos out of the 13.5 million on the platform, including mine. Reba Rocket from Takedown Piracy and Bennet Kelley of Internet Law Center also helped remove the video from the remaining websites refusing to do so.*

After hearing the news, I wanted to release the guttural scream I'd swallowed down for decades. I waited for a surge of relief. Instead, I was met with numbness. To survive my ordeal, I'd built calcified walls to deaden and protect myself. Perhaps it was terror that if I ever allowed that fury to finally erupt, I'd never be able to stop shrieking.

Nothing could change the fact that millions had already seen the video, arguably worse than the assault itself.

---

* More than twenty-five years after my assault, I'm still finding copies of my assault video online and working to purge it from the web. After these measures, it's easy to remove the video from most well-known porn sites. But there are still hundreds of links online, and many websites remain unresponsive. The statute of limitations has passed for any legal recourse. I've explored contacting other women from the video for a possible class action civil lawsuit but found it impossible to find contact information. (Please reach out to me if you are one of these women.) I'll probably have to search hardcore porn sites periodically for the rest of my life to check if my assault video has been reuploaded.

BUNNIES

My idol, Sung-Hi Lee, shot regularly with *Playboy*'s Kim Mizuno, who was integral to her fame. He photographed most of her iconic *Playboy* spreads and covers, her calendar, and her *Butterfly* coffee table photo book. His East Meets West calendar was the gold standard of Asian model calendars. I owned the 1998 sixteen-month calendar, measuring eleven by fourteen inches and printed on premium glossy paper. I studied it like a bible on pinup posing techniques. Sung-Hi graced the cover in a portrait shot, highlighting her elegant face and cleavage, perfectly tucked into a silver bikini top. Also appearing that year were Asian heritage *Playboy* greats such as Alley Baggett, Lisa Marie Scott, and Lola Corwin.

Eager to follow in Sung-Hi's footsteps, about a month after shooting with Julie Strain, I submitted photos to Mizuno. A week later, I showed up to his Los Angeles studio dolled up and glimmering with hope. Mizuno, a half-Black-and-Japanese man of average build, opened the door and welcomed me in. He was friendly and inviting without being the least bit creepy.

"I'll shoot some stills to submit to *Playboy*," he said, motioning to the bathroom for changing. "Let's shoot a couple bikini shots first."

I whipped off my clothing in the bathroom, changing into a shiny gold bikini. He flicked on lights in front of the white backdrop and took a few quick snaps with his camera as I posed, first with my front facing him and then my back.

"Okay, now with everything off," he said, turning around to give me a bit of privacy. I tossed my bikini into my purse and stood for the quick shots. The entire shoot took no more than five minutes.

"Okay, great, I'll let you know what they say," he said as I headed out. It was perhaps my quickest audition ever. I didn't know what to think. Perhaps it went horribly or perhaps it didn't.

By the time I got the call for a shoot with Mizuno for the August 2000 *Playboy Special Edition*, I had almost lost hope since the response took so long. On the day of the shoot, I woke up at 5:30 a.m. to prepare for the trek over to a mansion in Topanga Canyon for the 7:00 a.m. call time. I nervously dabbed Wet n Wild concealer onto my bruised legs; I was clumsy and always crashing into wall corners and bedposts. In front of the camera, my awkwardness usually melted away, but that day I faltered. I felt self-conscious of my wide nose, my long forehead, and the stretch marks on my outer thighs. I knew I had only a fraction of Sung-Hi's beauty, with her miniature dab of a nose and perfectly proportioned heart of a face. I was just a low-rent replica.

My nerves magnified after learning that I would be paired

with a stranger: Vietnamese model Thai Anh. The theme was "Girlfriends," and the concept was women performing lesbianism. It was assumed that we could act sexually voracious for each other. I'm heterosexual and felt awkward feigning sexual attraction for a woman. Thai also appeared nonplussed about sharing her *Playboy* appearance with me. During the shoot, we spoke only during introductions. We were uncomfortable, with no idea of proper hand placement, barely touching. The resulting photo was practically sexless. We smiled like acquaintances who happened to be naked together at the same time, not looking at each other in any way sexually. In comparison, the import models Sasha Singleton—later one of Mizuno's favorites—and Angela Alanis also appeared in the same issue, except their photos sizzled. Their hands are all over each other, tearing clothing, their teeth bared.

I didn't love the final photos. They just reminded me of Sung-Hi's vast superiority. She fell into modeling at age eighteen while attending Ohio State University, scouted by an agency. After a chance meeting with a *Playboy* photographer, who submitted her Polaroids to the magazine, she shot for *Playboy*. She wasn't even interested in posing at first and had no modeling aspirations, but the photographer hounded her for six months until she agreed to a photo shoot. The shoot turned out so well that the magazine booked her again as one of the fifteen models featured in its "The Girls of Hawaiian Tropic" issue. From there, she quickly became one of the most popular *Playboy Special Edition* models. I, on the other hand, had to practically break down doors to get my foot through. No one was asking me to appear in the magazine. I was begging them to feature me. I weaseled my way in once, but Mizuno and *Playboy* never asked me to shoot again (though the photos from that shoot were reprinted in future issues and I was later in a *Playboy* video).

In the end, I achieved only a fraction of Sung-Hi's success. The "Girlfriends" spread was the only flat I shot for, never reaching Playmate status or gracing the cover like Sung-Hi. And though the photos weren't great, that they were printed in this magazine was a huge deal to me. I could call myself a *Playboy* model. As a teenager, I'd actively pursued friendships with girls hotter than me, in hopes that the attention on them would blanket me as well. Being in an issue of *Playboy* was the same. It seemed natural that if my photos were slotted in between photos of stunning women, some of that gleam would glitter on me, giving me an instant status boost.

Playboy Enterprises was the kingpin of early aughts "raunch culture" (a phrase coined by Ariel Levy in *Feminist Chauvinist Pigs*), with the hit television show *The Girls Next Door* teaching young women to aspire to be sugar baby wives for a septuagenarian misogynist. I, along with many women in my generation, worshipped at the altar of *Playboy,* even as post-feminists. These misogynistic ideals resonated deeply with that little girl who was invisible to her father and the boys at school.

Like a mindless, hypnotized concert crowd, we propped Hugh Hefner's empire high in outstretched hands, forgetting feminist predecessors and icons I genuinely respected like Gloria Steinem, who boycotted magazines like his just a few decades prior. Maybe we conveniently forgot because *Playboy* could catapult a woman to mainstream success. After all, *Baywatch,* the biggest show on television with more than 1.1 billion viewers in 142 countries at its peak in 1996, featured a bevy of bouncing Playmates throughout its run, including Pamela Anderson, Donna D'Errico, Erika Eleniak, and Carmen Electra.

At the end of the twentieth century, porn culture had become mainstream. We thought we were relishing in the fruits of sexual freedom and fully controlling our bodies and narratives. Between the Girls Gone Wild commercials, which became inescapable on late-night television, and *Maxim, FHM,* and *Stuff*—popular men's magazines featuring scores of scantily clad women—it was a considerable coup to appear on the pages of these magazines, and young women thought themselves powerful. During this period, models and pop stars normalized and celebrated the shedding of clothing. Many Gen X Asian women like me were itching to flout stereotypes of the studious, nerdy Asian, dropping their inhibitions and creating internet content that made Asian fetishization readily accessible.

I was thrilled to hold the title of *FHM* Student of the Year in 2001, with a glossy full-page feature in the magazine. Leslie Bibb—a legitimate actress—graced the magazine cover, naked except for a white sheet. Despite the less-than-flattering blurb accompanying my feature, which snarked that I bragged about being bilingual and getting good grades yet missed half the random quiz questions they threw at me, I still took pride in my defiance against the model minority trope, albeit halfheartedly. As a collective we set the scene for the oncoming onslaught of Asian pinup models. Nude women on the internet proliferated, but entering *Playboy* model status meant joining an elite group—akin to earning a pageant title.

I even added television credits to my résumé and found an acting agent. I wasn't particularly passionate about acting, but almost every pinup model aspired to go "legit" with an acting career, and I followed suit. I was cast on *The Man Show*, which premiered in 1999 and was billed as "a joyous celebration of chauvinism." I appeared more than once as one of the nameless and uncredited bikini-clad trampoline girls featured in the end credits of each episode. We, along with my fellow pinups and *Playboy* models, were in a collective hypnotic state, not realizing that the gorgeously ripe, shiny red apple of sexual freedom we were relishing was filled with worms; we were purging ourselves of feminist achievements and sending ourselves backward.

These institutions not only encouraged the objectification of women; they propagated the Asian fetish, dedicating entire issues and videos to scantily clad Asian women bouncing about. In 2000, *Playboy* released a special newsstand edition called "*Playboy's* Asian Beauties," and before that, in 1998, the *Asian Exotica* DVD. The description for the DVD reads: "The mystique of the Asian woman is one of the world's most alluring fantasies," adding further descriptives such as "erotic rituals of the exotic Far East" and "celebration of the Orient."

Many of my website photo sets at the time played directly into this perceived exoticism of Asian women with fans, qipaos, and paper umbrellas, as if it were essential to appear visibly Asian. One of my most popular photo sets has me wearing a scandalized version of a qipao, also known as a cheongsam. It's scarlet, snug, and strapless, with a high slit revealing generous swaths of thigh. Unlike the traditional ankle-length qipao with capped sleeves and a high neck, which protect a woman's modesty, my dress fell midthigh and had no sleeves or neckline; it covered no more than a towel does coming out of the shower. My face is soft and inviting.

I felt radiant that day, with my hair pulled into a high ponytail and topped with a red flower, while crouching elegantly atop a gold embroidered dining chair. Over a series of photos, my dress slinks lower and lower down my body. Soon I'm topless, but I never completely remove the dress, as I do in other photo sets where I'm not wearing anything stereotypical. When playing into my Asian features, I couldn't altogether remove the qipao—my racial drag.

Asiaphiles don't stop at fetishizing our features; they crave an unmistakably Asian image, cloaked in traditional baubles and exotic symbols like our authenticity needs to be enhanced to satisfy their fantasy. It's as if we're cast in a play and only allowed to perform the part of the simpering Asian woman—something that was apparent in the comments on my fan sites at the start of my modeling career. My manager's assistant remembers seeing many remarks on my Yahoo fan group about wanting to dress me up in geisha garb, eating sushi off my naked body, and penetrating me with chopsticks, both highlighting my Asianness and relegating me to a sex toy. This obsession with highlighting an Asian woman's ethnicity is perfectly illustrated in the 1962 movie *The World of Suzie Wong* set in Hong Kong—a product of British imperialism. Hong Kong was considered a gentleman's playground with sexually available China dolls. The eponymous lead, played by Nancy Kwan, wears a multitude of stunning formfitting and high-slitted qipaos. In one memorable scene, Suzie is lustrous in an embroidered white silk diyi—ceremonial dress reserved for Chinese empresses. She's pure grace under the waterfall of flower-dotted fabric. Topped with a golden crown of dangling jeweled chains, Wong kneels and bows her head to her lover, Robert Lomax, played by the aging heartthrob William Holden. He's speechless when she appears in traditional Chinese garb, and they melt into an extended romantic kiss. The scene contrasts sharply with an earlier one in which Suzie wears what I personally thought was a classy outfit, like something one might wear to brunch at Tiffany's. Her white floral dress is paired with open-toed blue pumps and a black birdcage veil partially covering her face. Robert is pure fury, saying she looks like a "cheap European streetwalker," and aggressively tears the dress off her. For him, the very elegant white dress dampens her Asianness, making her less appealing. She's only fuckable and lovable when she stays within the confines of his Orientalist standards, much like when I was a kid and never received the same validation in the strappy sundresses and fluttery skirts from Wet Seal my blond-haired white friends did.

It wasn't until I emulated the centuries of stereotypical recycled fantasies from the media, cloaking my face and body to enhance myself as an Asian woman, that the likes, clicks, and views on my photos increased exponentially. At first, eroticizing Asian accessories, clothing, and cultural props was a cheap and hackneyed way to highlight my difference from other women simply wearing lingerie and bikinis and to elevate myself above the pack. These accoutrements seemed cheeky, a playful way to get men to notice me. I didn't realize then that I was reinforcing my otherness at the expense of my self-worth and the identities of women who looked like me. The attention was intoxicating, and even if I had to play into the stereotype of the supine Asian woman, I felt impregnable.

Now, it's humbling to realize that I had to lean into my Asianness while Sung-Hi never did. Even though she has posed as a schoolgirl, I never saw her drape herself in overtly Asian props to emphasize her mystique. It wasn't necessary because she was beautiful just as she was. Her success was prolific, untouched by qipaos, fans, or tiny umbrellas. Meanwhile, I strived relentlessly to emulate her but was just a wannabe thrift store caricature.

———

Not long after my failed *Playboy* "Girlfriends" shoot, I got the call for another dream photo shoot. As a paying subscriber to Sung-Hi's website, I visited it often. On the home page, her fans were greeted with a photo of Sung-Hi perched on a bed of green leaves with a cavalcade of limbs crossed over her body in what's known as an implied nude—naked, but all the naughty bits are covered. Bursting from her naked back were transparent blue butterfly wings, and below, two Flash-enabled monarch butterflies waved in welcome. Photoshopped buttons with cursive text encircled her, inviting clicks to navigate to other sections of her website. It was a classy website cover page, elegant even. One day, I noticed she'd added a new "Model Discoveries" section. I immediately clicked the contact button below Sung-Hi's perfect little feet and emailed a selection of photos. *This could be my big break,* I thought. At this point, I was a junior in college and had shaved off ten pounds, blossoming into my looks. My confidence had ratcheted up since my junior high days.

In my email, I told her my name was Kaila Yu. I never considered using my legal name, Elaine Yang, when I started modeling. I always thought it sounded like an old lady's name, and I needed to hide my modeling pursuits from my mother, who was certain to oppose this life choice. I picked my last name for this new alter ego first, thinking it'd be cute to use a play on my boyfriend Don's last name, subconsciously marrying him even though I never cared about marriage. He was incredibly supportive of my modeling career and eagerly offered to snap the nudes I submitted to Sung-Hi. I thought I was the luckiest girl in the world. (Although in retrospect, don't most guys discourage their girlfriends from posing nude?) I wanted to show him I was grateful in my own way. For my new first name, I cycled through a few options. At first, I used Li-Ting, to imitate Sung-Hi, even going as far as purchasing the domain name litingyu.com. The name didn't feel quite right, but one of my favorite Filipino American boy groups was called Kai. Their saccharine love song "Say You'll Stay" was on repeat on my iPod. As an homage, my name became Kaila, which I liked because it sounded ethnically ambiguous—Hawaiian or Asian. Elaine was now dead.

Later that week, as I pulled into Don's driveway where I lived with his family in Walnut, a voicemail notification from an unknown number appeared on my clear Nokia cell phone.

"Hey, Kaila," said the recording. "This is Sung-Hi. I got your photos and would love to feature you on my website. My photographer will be in contact with further details."

I yelped inside my black Toyota Celica, suddenly dizzy. "This is Sung-Hi," she had said on my voicemail. The woman I had idolized for years had called me!

"Don!" I shouted, running upstairs to the bedroom. "Listen to this!"

I replayed the message to my boyfriend. He smirked, self-satisfied and proud. "See? I knew she would call." He later bragged about it to all his friends, and I saved Sung-Hi's voicemail for years.

Weeks later, I showed up at a perfectly manicured mansion in the Hollywood Hills, clutching a bag of freshly purchased lingerie for the photo shoot. That day I met Sung-Hi in person, but it was nothing like I imagined. She looked just as stunning as her photos but was formally polite with a taut smile—like a morning news anchor sick of her job. I'd fantasized she'd tuck me under her wing as a mentee. I asked to shoot a photo set together.

"Oh, I don't do that," she replied, politely lying to blow me off. I knew she'd previously shot photo sets with her best friend, the popular *Playboy* model Lisa Boyle, and emerging model Linda Tran.

In person, Sung-Hi was nothing like the sexy, honey-sweet vixen on film (something others would later echo about me). At that moment, she was attempting to transition into acting, following the road map of *Playboy* Playmates Pamela Anderson and Jenny McCarthy. Hollywood was the natural next step in her career. Although Sung-Hi was never a Playmate, she achieved a notable career high as the first solo Asian *Playboy* cover girl in 1996. That issue, featuring her headshot with perfectly orbed cleavage peeking out of a white pushup bra, was one of my most prized possessions. She's wide-eyed with heavily dusted crescents of navy eyeshadow, her fingers grasping a thick mane of tousled hair. Sung-Hi is breathtakingly striking, but in retrospect, her expression seems more grimace than welcoming, eyes deadened like a robotic sex doll.

Several years earlier, she had published *Butterfly*, a gorgeously lush hardcover photo book of elegant nudes shot by Mizuno. It was an instant bestseller in Korea until it was banned. That same year, 1997, more than three thousand fans showed up for the book signing of her new biography, *Yellow Butterfly of Hollywood*. Her acting career was also on the rise. She starred in *A Night on the Water* in 1998 and *Error in Judgment* in 1999 and guest-starred on four episodes of the television series *Mortal Kombat: Conquest*. Sung-Hi wanted to escape pinup modeling, not baby a wannabe butterfly like me.

As I arrived on site, a lady with flowing dirty-blond hair opened the mansion's heavily carved wooden door. She looked like a former flower child from the 1970s. "You must be Kaila. I'm Victoria, your makeup artist," she chirped, her gentle disposition instantly calming.

"That's me," I replied shyly, looking at the floor.

I watched as she transformed me in the mirror, basting my face in thick layers of foundation, concealer, base powder, and finishing powder. Next, the pièce de résistance: Victoria pulled out feathery, thick swaths of fake eyelashes and carefully trimmed them with tiny scissors to fit my eyes.

"Now look down and try not to blink," she said while blowing on the applied glue.

I stared downward obediently as she gently tapped the voluminous lashes atop my nonexistent ones. After they dried, I looked up at myself in the mirror.

"Wow," we said breathlessly in unison. My eyes had popped wide open. The lashes had completely transformed my face in a far more dramatic way than I could've imagined.

Next, she added volume to my sparse head of hair. "Let's give you some hair, baby," Victoria joked as she whipped out a bag full of wigs and extensions. She reached strategically into my scalp and clipped on what felt like five pounds of hair pieces onto my meager strands.

Victoria's work was a revelation. By the time she finished, my upper and lower eyelids had been lined with thick strokes of black kohl, and my face had been dusted all over with her magical brush. My hair, now thick and obsidian, cascaded down to my hips; it weighed heavily, like a fourteen-karat gold crown with all the power of Samson, a sparkling shield over my self-consciousness. I had been transformed from skinny little girl into smoky-eyed vamp. I now had glinting cat eyes, perfectly shaded with conspicuous flourishes of prismatic glitter shadow, and overlined and glossy lips. That day, I experienced firsthand that beauty was a weapon—a counterpunch to all that self-hate I'd internalized in my youth. It didn't matter if it was manufactured.

I smiled at my reflection in the mirror. Growing up, I had been Elaine. Elaine was the introvert, the nerd, the "total dog." Kaila would step up in stilettos and kick Elaine to the curb. Kaila would gleam with confidence. She was liquid gold. Kaila would reign over the world of celluloid digitization, her images transformed into MPEGs and JPEGs—compressed, and photoshopped, and endlessly replicated onto hard drives. She would become the next Sung-Hi Lee, adored and beloved by thousands of men and immortalized online.

And then there were two of us. Kaila and Elaine. I had transformed into the *butterfly*.

EXOTIC

A year into modeling, I found myself growing increasingly insecure about my face, especially my eyes. In those early photos, I'm wide-eyed, but not because I was trying to look innocent. It wasn't submission. I'd been conditioned to believe that bigger eyes meant desirability. During summer vacations in Taiwan as a teenager, I loved getting dolled up for Taiwanese-style glamour shots, where photographers would coach me to widen my eyes, insisting that bigger eyes were a mark of beauty. In my professional model photos, I was consciously forcing my eyes to appear larger, as I'd been taught, convinced it increased my attractiveness. My natural eyes felt too small, too sleepy, not the doe-eyed ideal I longed for. Though I had a natural epithelial fold, my eyes didn't resemble the large, exaggerated anime eyes I coveted.

Back in Taiwan, my aunt took me to the convenience store Watsons to purchase eyelid tape when I was upset with my resulting glamour photos. Women in Asia used these eyelid-shaping stickers—sold in sheets throughout 7-Elevens, malls, and night markets—placing them directly above the eyelid fold to stretch it higher and deeper. But I didn't know where to buy eyelid tape in the United States and I never placed it correctly. I needed a better solution to make my eyes pop, to make them look brighter, larger, and more expressive.

Bigger eyes were the ideal, so I wanted them. I've never heard of anyone wishing for smaller eyes. I wasn't trying to look white, but there's no denying I was shaped by American media, where blond hair and blue eyes reigned supreme as the ultimate beauty standard. As a child, I envied white friends with their large, expressive eyes speaking volumes in a single glance. The insidious pull of internalized racism led me to subconsciously covet white features, upheld as superior, while my own felt inadequate. Growing up, I witnessed racists making fun of Asian eyes, placing the tips of their fingers to their temples and pulling their eyes into ugly slits. I refused to be the butt of this joke, so I went under the knife again, this time slicing my eyelids to create deeper folds to exaggerate my eyes open.

This procedure is known as blepharoplasty, or, colloquially, eyelid surgery. Eyelid surgery was popularized by a white man who had specific judgments on the Asian face. In the 1950s, while Dr. Ralph Millard was stationed in Seoul during the Korean War, he experimented with creating an eyelid fold on local women. In the *American Journal of Ophthalmology,* Millard wrote that the monolid "gives the effect of an expressionless eye sneaking a peep through a slit, a characteristic which through fact and fiction has become associated with mystery and intrigue." He said, "The absence of the puerperal fold produces a passive expression which seems to epitomize the stoical and unemotional manner of the oriental." It seems he considered Asians subhuman and incapable of true emotions and that fixing their monolids created an illusion of human feeling.

The racist implications of Millard's invention are obvious. Approximately 50 percent of Asians have monolids—eyelids with no crease. Those with creases are considered "lucky" and considered the standard of Asian beauty. Millard's goal was to make Korean prostitutes more attractive to American soldiers and to help "war brides" become more Americanized and assimilable, working in tandem with the War Brides Act of 1945, which allowed Korean and Japanese women married to American soldiers to immigrate to the United States. Many of these women underwent the same surgery to assimilate and appear nonthreatening, as interracial marriage was still illegal in some parts of the United States until 1967, according to Claire Lee in a 2015 article for *The Korean Herald* titled "Uncovering the History of Double Eyelid Surgery."

The logic was that the surgery would allow war brides to appear less "other" as foreigners. That the surgery was practiced on prostitutes to increase their attractiveness to American soldiers suggests these men preferred doe-eyed Asian women as well. Millard found smaller, slantier eyes threatening because they were too "foreign," but many fetishists revel in the enigmatic exoticism of monolids, believing they convey passivity. It's a double-edged sword, boxing Asian women into a corner. We're striving for Western standards of larger-eyed beauty yet fetishized for almond-shaped eyes.

Interestingly, double eyelid surgery doesn't fundamentally

change the shape of the eye—it widens it. Cat eyes, often almond shaped and slightly slanted, are never considered small and expressionless the way Asian eyes are. In effect, the surgery actually transforms Asian eyes to be more catlike, further emphasizing us as animalistic, seductive, and exotic. Much like breast augmentation, it simply co-opts Western ideals, "accidentally" making Asian women even more enticing to fetishists. With larger yet still slanted eyes, these surgically modified eyes evoke mystique with the addition of infantilized innocence—both traits fetishized under yellow fever.

To fetishists, the "slant" is alluring, foreign, and mysterious. "You're so exotic" is a common "compliment" given by Asiaphiles. One definition of *exotic*, from the *Cambridge Dictionary*, reads "unusual and exciting because of coming (or seeming to come) from far away, especially a tropical country." With the myth of the Asian woman, the word *exotic* teams heightened overt sexualization with ideas of foreign, alien, and other, like a rare captured creature men can brag about in an attempt to enhance their virility. Our slanted "almond" eyes differentiate us, and sex-crazed men seek us out to fulfill their basest fantasies. Another online dictionary definition of exotic is "originating in or characteristic of a distant foreign country." Calling Asian women exotic highlights white beauty standards as the norm and Asian women are the deviation. It's a microaggression, saying our beauty doesn't fit the mainstream white lens, and a way of asserting dominance. We're not rugs, plants, birds, or objects, and we don't need special categories separate from conventional white beauty standards. It's dehumanizing and insulting.

"You're so exotic" is usually followed by "Where are you from?" even though many of us are born in the United States. All women have experienced objectification, but the addition of race strips away our humanity. The obsession with our eyes, vaginas, and silky black hair reduces us to unusually strange and fantastical sex objects. This obsession with Asian features devalues individuals, as these same features are found in almost all Asian women. Notice that the word *exotic* is used frequently to describe Asian women versus *pretty* or *beautiful*, a compliment commonly given to white women. We're a curiosity, and there's a thinly veiled carnal connotation. Instead of beautiful, you're insinuating that we're sexually subservient geisha.

Throughout my youthful modeling career, I often leaned into exoticism, relishing how it made me feel unique, not realizing I was allowing myself to be viewed in a reductive and derogatory lens. I was also genuinely proud of being Asian, and growing up feeling marginalized, I felt emphasizing my Asianness was like a celebration of my culture. At the time, I unknowingly romanticized yellow fever, not understanding I was playing into an aesthetic rooted in centuries of Orientalized objectification.

Exotification of Asian women dates to the early nineteenth century with Afong Moy, known as the Chinese Lady, a curiosity who toured the States as a sideshow exhibition, drawing large crowds. Arriving in 1834 and said to be only fourteen, she was a novelty before mass Chinese immigration to the States and possibly the first Chinese woman to step foot in America. With her teeny bound feet, exhibitors relished in her delicate otherness—a racialized and sexualized object.

In *Marginal Sights: Staging the Chinese in America*, the theater professor James S. Moy (no relation) interpreted her viewings as "a grand panoptic event which no doubt offered to the gaze of the spectator a sense of empowerment ... exclusively for the sake of audience amusement." Like a docile zoo creature, Afong Moy displayed herself to riveted crowds dressed in sumptuous Chinese embroidered silks while acting out her supposed daily routine, eating rice and drinking tea in a glass box—like a butterfly trapped in a transparent jar. She reportedly spent four to five hours daily perfecting this exotic persona for her white audience.

With her onyx hair combed back and disciplined with gold pins and flowers, she dressed nothing like the average Chinese. Instead, she was lavishly cloaked in yellow, green, and red gold-embroidered gowns to entertain her white audience. It's believed she went on to inspire the first performance using yellowface—a Hollywood tradition of white actors using makeup and costumes to appear Asian, common in the late 1800s to the mid-1900s (one of the defining aspects was the taping of eyes back to appear exaggeratedly slanted)* —at a Washington masquerade, according to Tao Zhang in his essay "The Start of American Accommodation of the Chinese: Afong Moy's Experience from 1834 to 1850." Moy's career ended around 1950, and she disappeared from all public records, with no death certificate or mention in a census. Like with

---

* Although the practice of yellowface has faded, a new "fox eyes" trend went viral on TikTok in 2020. Women like Emma Chamberlain, Gigi Hadid, and Kendall Jenner used makeup to create the appearance of slanted Asian eyes. That alone wasn't problematic, but the final photo of the look was often paired with the women's fingers pulling back at their temples to create the slant, the same racist gesture thrown at Asians, taunting them for having ugly, "chinky" eyes. These women were appropriating our eyes but never had to undergo the racist judgment we grew up with.

other bizarre creatures and circus acts, her fawning white audiences unceremoniously discarded her after their curiosity faded.

———

After consulting with Dr. Francis Sheng, who did my breast implants, I took the plunge. He said it was an easy surgery with minimal recovery time, and I was sold after reviewing his book of before and after photos. I went under general anesthesia, although the procedure is possible with local anesthesia. At the time, I was a druggie and enjoyed getting knocked out for surgery. Many people dread going under, but to me, instantly losing consciousness was a gift. I knew the inherent risks but never thought they would happen to me. I simply trusted my doctors. I feel this way even to this day.

After taking my vitals, my nurse told me to change into my robe. "Lie back and get cozy," she instructed, placing a heated blanket atop me. I felt like an infant, safe and coddled in the womb. "Let's look at your veins," she said as she prepped my arm for the IV and I pumped a squishy stress ball. "Hmm, your veins are tiny; this is going to be tough." She sounded vaguely concerned. This was something no one wants to hear, even though I'm not afraid of needles. "This is going to sting," she warned.

I took a deep breath as she gouged a needle deep into my vein. It hurt quite a bit, but only briefly, until I felt the cool liquid pulsating into my body, feeling instantly nourished. The nurse wheeled me into the operating room, the anesthesiologist and doctor greeting me with kind smiles.

"You're going to feel a burning sting, and before you know it, it'll all be over," my anesthesiologist said as she stuck a needle into the tube.

The fiery medicine infiltrating my veins stung more than expected, and as always, I tried to stay up as long as possible before passing out. I've never made it past five seconds. Before I could ask, "Is it supposed to burn this much?" I was out.

Dr. Sheng made full incisions above my double eyelids as I slept. It was a relatively easy surgery, taking a week to heal. My eyes stayed puffy for several weeks afterward. After the surgery and throughout the healing process, I felt accomplished. Every surgery had always felt like a positive transformation. As someone with multiple tattoos might say, that instant gratification is cathartic, addictive even. Going under the knife had the same effect for me. Each alteration erased a part of my old self and a piece of my trauma.

Cutting my eyelids was, perhaps, an attempt to carve away the racist perceptions of small, slanty eyes. All my other acts of rebellion unconsciously targeted the model minority myth, a silent protest against expectations of how I was supposed to behave because of my appearance. Obedient Asians, the ones who neatly fit this mold, had a stellar work ethic but weren't edgy, cool, or beautiful. They also had boring, expressionless eyes to match. And if I wanted to annihilate Elaine—that undesirable little girl—I had to erase my eyes.

After the surgery, I felt even more like Kaila than Elaine. Elaine was shy and boring—the typical nerdy model minority. Wide-eyed Kaila burst into the world with a knowing smile and playful glint in her eye.

RACE QUEENS

I hadn't set out to become an import model (a pinup style of model for the tuner car scene)—my idol, Sung-Hi Lee, was never one—but as soon as I gained notoriety online, requests poured in from import car parts companies eager to hire me. Never one to pass up an opportunity, I attended my first import car show in the early 2000s. Dressed in a slinky blue knit top from Melrose Avenue and a white skirt that hugged my curves, I was unprepared for the distance from the parking lot to Del Mar Fairgrounds, teetering in my transparent platform stilettos—the ones strippers dance in. Luckily, scantily clad young women could skip the lines snaking around the block.

I entered the hall, which throbbed with loud thumping bass, to a packed floor of attendees sporting baggy jeans and zero fades, decked-out vendor booths lined with preening models, and candy-colored cars slammed (lowering the car suspension to look sportier) to the ground and graffitied with stickers. I was armed with a stack of glossy four-by-six flyers advertising my new paid-membership website—the old-school version of OnlyFans. The photo on the front was an elegant profile shot from my shoot for Sung-Hi's website. In it, I'm leaning against a Greek-inspired column on the patio of a rented mansion in the Hollywood Hills with my back arched. I'm topless, but strategically placed hair covers all the naughty bits. In the photo, all I'm wearing are hair extensions and a tiny blue thong. I was prepared to hand out flyers to the attendees and gain more subscribers, but the power of this tight-knit subculture and exposure from Sung-Hi's website and *Playboy* magazine meant many already knew me.

"*Kay-la,*" someone shouted, pronouncing my name wrong. "Can I take a photo with you?"

The moment I arrived, fans rushed up, octopusing arms around my waist, often slipping their hands slightly lower than appropriate. I gritted my teeth in a smile while inwardly wincing at those scummy guys with wandering hands. A rush of photographers swarmed around me, their snapping cameras like thousands of clapping hands, but their sublime focus on me was short-lived.

"Oh, shit, it's Tiara," shouted one of the photographers. Suddenly the horde of men swarmed away from me toward a model sauntering through the car show, decked out in a red bustier top, matching frilly panties, white thigh-high stockings, and clear stilettos like the ones I had on. She had a full head of glossy auburn hair with bangs and perky C-cups. She was Thai and Korean, her mixed heritage making her instantly more exotic and desirable. The crowd parted for her and her big Samoan bodyguard, Abe, and a sea of guys trailed after her as if she were a lingerie-clad pied piper. The crowds marched past me, leaving me in her glittery wake. In the world of import models, fans are forever chasing the shiniest new thing, discarding the old as soon as something more sparkly comes in view.

———

The import subculture originated in the late '80s and early '90s. Asian youth started modifying Honda Civics, Toyota MR2s, and other imported four- and six-cylinder Japanese cars, known as JDMs (Japanese domestic market). Many were customized weathered automobiles passed down by parents or vehicles affordable enough for twentysomethings to purchase. For these young Asian men, the import scene allowed them to establish a masculine identity, a counterculture to the nerdy Asian male stereotype proliferating in the media, like the cringe character Takashi in *Revenge of the Nerds* (1984) and *Revenge of the Nerds III: The Next Generation* (1992).

Ironically, through the process of asserting Asian American masculinity, young men reverted to traditional male gender roles and female subordination. It's impossible to ignore gender inequalities in any car culture, including the import scene. At the start, Asian men composed the vast majority of attendees and participants at the events, many actively rebelling against the model minority myth. Hip-hop culture was a dominant influence, with Asian males acting "gangsta" and speaking in African American Vernacular English (AAVE). Also borrowed was rap music's degradation and subjugation of women as sex objects.

Asian women didn't have much presence in the import scene beyond being scantily clad adornments, not too different from custom decals, rims, body kits, or snazzy paint jobs. They were meant to be decorations but quickly dominated the scene, becoming the main draw for many attendees, who came to leer and ogle at women instead of cars.

We were hunted by camera lenses capturing trophies of sexual imagery to mount on computer screens like deer antlers over a fireplace. At the time, I thought this attention was the ultimate empowerment, but the men had all the ammo to knock me off my pedestal. There were always dozens of younger, fresher Asian models ready and willing to take my place. Many female car show attendees were underage girls in skimpy clothing, vying for camera time and dreaming of becoming import models themselves. According to Soo Ah Kwon in "Autoexoticizing: Asian American Youth and the Import Car Scene," roughly 35 percent of import car show attendees were female and were mainly girlfriends of import fans, models, or aspiring models. Import models were also instrumental in mainstreaming the ABG (Asian baby girl) aesthetic.

Car shows like Hot Import Nights, Import Showoff, Extreme AutoFest, Battle of the Imports, and the NOPI shows were among the biggest in the United States, competing with NASCAR. The tuner market gained momentum, reaching all-time highs by 2000. The car shows served as an Asian American cultural and social event for men to show off their cars, hang out, assert Asian pride, and check out models. A typical Hot Import Nights event in Southern California during what would become known as the "golden age of tuning" was the event of the year for local Asian Americans, drawing five hundred cars and twenty-five thousand people. It was more like a club event, taking place in the evening and including DJs, live performances, breakdancing competitions, and bikini contests. These Skittles-colored cars brought an air of cool culture and united Asian Americans in likely the first cohesive movement across the country.

Drivers from our scene got endorsement deals, tuners graced the silver screen, and import models started to break into the mainstream. During this time, *Import Tuner* magazine started featuring models on its covers. You could find the magazine next to *Newsweek* or *Vogue* in the checkout aisle of the grocery store but more likely next to men's magazines, like *FHM* or *Maxim*, featuring objectified and sexualized images of women.

To be considered a legitimate model and not a wannabe, you had to appear on the cover of *Import Tuner*. The first issue of *Import Tuner* debuted in 1998 with the Remix Twins on the cover, the first famous, or what I'd call "name," import models. Jennifer and Olivia Clarin were Filipina twins and members of a dance crew. Most famously, the twins danced in the Notorious B.I.G.'s "Hypnotize" music video; that song and video were inescapable then. This was before the internet and hundreds of cable television channels, so being in a music video airing on MTV was monumental. Print magazines also had a far more significant impact back then. *Import Tuner* was a spinoff of *Turbo Magazine* and the first magazine to realize the massive driving force import models had on the industry. *Import Tuner* always featured a model and a car on the cover, while the magazine's content concerned itself with car modification tips. It also published the iconic import car–themed comic strip *Max Boost!* by Dennis Caco. For those who couldn't attend a car show, there was a section in the back recapping the top shows across the country, including photos of cars and top models. That first generation of *Import Tuner* covers became collectibles, still sold on eBay today.

I was ecstatic when I received the email to shoot for the November 2000 cover in my first year of entering the industry. On shoot day, it was exhilarating to have a stylist; they were rarely provided for import shoots. Instead, many of us would lug around a suitcase filled with bikinis, lingerie sets, and costumes packed neatly in Ziploc bags for easy accessibility. I'd already envisioned my cover shoot months before I got the offer. I wanted to wear something tight and pink, with pigtails—my signature go-to look and a fan favorite. I looked young and innocent and leaned into the underage aesthetic. Instead, I was given a side ponytail and handed an army-green crop top, cargo pants, and tan kicks. It's not what I would've chosen, but I'll admit, it was much more stylish than what I had in mind. I strutted onto set confidently.

I was no longer the scared little girl cowering instead of modeling for Kim Mizuno; I now had hundreds of paying website subscribers. Sung-Hi's webmaster, Misha, had invited me to join her family of sites. It was prestigious because she managed the websites of only three models—the other two being *Playboy* Playmate Shae Marks and *Playboy* star Lisa Boyle—all of them sweepingly high above me in stature. My newly Misha-designed site had gone live on October 17, 2000.

I confidently moved through my poses with calculated precision. Male fans would often ask what ran through my head while modeling, expecting an answer confirming their fantasies. I knew what they wanted—something to whet their sexual appetite as if I were an animatronic, built for lust. The truth was far less titillating. I just wanted to hit the correct poses, finish, and go home. I didn't enjoy the act of modeling. It was the published photos I adored, the ones existing forever in print.

"Can I get on top of the car?" I asked.

"Oh," the photographer replied, surprised. "Let me ask." He left to whisper to the stylist and art director before returning. "Okay, we can try, but please be very careful."

I climbed onto the car's hood and quickly nailed the pose before sliding off, to the relief of everyone. My instinct was right, and a picture from that series of poses wound up on the cover, and to this day, it's one of my favorite photos. I'm perched atop the silver Honda S2000, and my expression is flirty, confident, and powerful. I still get comments from S2000 owners today, like, "I can't believe the owner let you get on the hood of their car!" I didn't realize that the thousands of dollars of modifications on the delicate hood are easily dented.

For the next few months, I was the darling of the import scene . . . until Tiara's issue of *Import Tuner* came out. Her outfit left little to the imagination, highlighting her perfect C-cups, as she gazed seductively yet nonchalantly from the page—an electric but effortless beauty. Her cover is widely regarded as one of the best of all time, and she was invited back to shoot with other top models for the anniversary issue. Proud as I was of my cover shoot, it was my first and last time shooting for the magazine.

A mutual import model friend once said, "Tiara has the most beautiful face, and you have the best body in the business." She thought she was paying me a compliment, but I felt she was calling me a butterface and it struck a nerve. It reminded me of the fans who met me and frequently exclaimed, "Wow, you're so photogenic!" They didn't mean to insult me, but the subtext was clear: I looked better in photos than in person. I'd smile back weakly, but the competitive jealousy I felt magnified. Tiara was simply more alluring, and I was powerless. That helplessness blanketed me, thick and undeniable.

Yet being the hottest new model in the import scene, even for a moment, was intoxicating. The import car show scene dovetailed with the emerging Asian American club scene. For the next several years, weekends had me touring nightclubs and car shows nationwide. It was heady and exhilarating; we'd regularly make thousands of dollars in cash on top of our booking fees for selling our own posters and calendars.

Most of the top models of my generation were also hired to shoot for Namco's multiplatform racing video game *Street Racing Syndicate*. In 2004, it was released for PlayStation 2, GameCube, and Xbox. It was designed to compete with the popular *Need for Speed: Underground 2* and based on illegal street racing.

The premise was simple. Gamers would participate in street races, winning import model girlfriends along the way. Each winning race scored players new girlfriends, unlocking their dancing videos. One online review called it *"Need for Speed,* but horny." In this game, young men could amass import model girlfriends like collectible trading cards. Eleven out of the eighteen women in the game are Asian, reinforcing Orientalist fantasies of Asian women as interchangeable objects and bodies, although this demographic breakdown would be accurate for the import scene where Asian American culture dominated. However, it's another example of the depersonalization of Asian women, having players collecting us like Pokémon instead of selecting just one as a girlfriend. After the game's release, it garnered a cult following.

On the day of my shoot for *Street Racing Syndicate,* the makeup artist on set didn't seem to have experience working with features like mine, and my makeup, with tints of orange eyeshadow, was awful. At an earlier shoot that week, another makeup artist berated me for sneaking into the bathroom to fix her work, so I left my makeup alone. I seethed at the fact that when the same makeup artist worked on Tiara, she looked as stunning as ever.

The shoot was an awkward experience. The entire crew and some models watched while I stood alone on a silvery metal floor against a green screen, waiting for the sound playback. Once the speakers started blasting hip-hop, I was instructed to dance sultrily. Each model had been instructed to bring three clothing changes and danced in various stages of undress. My looks were a tiny blue tank top with low-cut blue Frankie B jeans, a stretchy yellow-and-white-striped crop top and denim shorts, and a gold studded bikini. We started fully clothed (at least by import model standards), returned for a second scene in something more revealing, and finished our routine wiggling around in a bikini. I can't dance and was horrified by the awkward final videos. By contrast Tiara's dancing scenes from the video game looked effervescent. She flirtily teased the camera as if she were having the time of her life.

Though Tiara outshone me, yet again, I was still proud to be included in this elite group. I relished the fact that I was one of the harder models to win in the game, as if being a more unattainable prize made objectification acceptable.

Each model's screen listed her measurements like cattle on the auction block.

Mine read:

Stats: 32-24-33

Height: 5'4"

Weight: 105 lbs

Info: Kaila loves guys who are a challenge, strong, and
    sensitive.

———

As the import scene gained popularity, mainstream media took notice, and import modeling quickly became the next media phenomenon catering to the yellow fever gaze, feeding it with always available and willing Asian woman. I didn't know a thing about cars, but I was happy to drape myself over expensive pieces of metal like a fresh paint job. I joined a generation of import models kicking off perhaps the most considerable proliferation of Asian pinup content for fetishists. Although attendance at import shows was primarily Asian, many models—including myself, Francine Dee, Natasha Yi, Felicia Tang, Tila Nguyen (later known as Tila Tequila), and more—had websites churning out weekly nude photo sets for thousands of mostly non-Asian men. Before the advent of the internet, Asiaphiles were limited to the obscure Asian specialty porn magazines. Now they enjoyed a deluge of content, with websites like Asian Sirens meticulously documenting and promoting the careers of import models. Busty Asian women aren't the norm, but we co-opted Western beauty standards, making us even more conventionally attractive.

This convergence of trends in the Asian community became such a full-blown pop culture phenomenon that Hollywood noticed, inspiring Universal Picture's most lucrative franchise, Fast & Furious—grossing $7.3 billion and counting. There were rumblings of excitement when rumors spread that an import tuning subculture movie was in development. Back in 2001, there weren't any successful street racing movies. With a $38 million budget, 2001's *The Fast and the Furious* was a love letter to import cars, making the cast into household names and eventually transforming the import industry. The only catch was that there was a dearth of Asians in the film except for Johnny Tran, the main villain, portrayed by Korean American Rick Yune. Asians were once again reduced to the sidelines in our own story, in the subculture we created.

Asian Americans in Southern California, especially, reacted negatively to the movie. Carter Jung, the former editor of *Import Tuner*, said in an interview with *Rise: A Pop History of Asian America from the Nineties to Now*, "When that movie first came out, I hated it. A lot of us in the industry did. The cars were ugly, the graphics were over the top. Plus, where were the Asians? This was *our* culture, and we were erased."

Despite the backlash, the Fast & Furious series went on to become one of Hollywood's most successful franchises. A 2002 *Los Angeles Times* article detailed that just ten years earlier, souped-up import cars had the derogatory nickname "rice rockets." But since the release of *The Fast and the Furious*, these cars have become ubiquitous across the United States, not just in enclaves with a high percentage of Asians like Irvine, home to the University of California, Irvine—nicknamed the University of Civics and Integras.

Over the course of the series, more Asians appeared in the films, but Asian women were never main characters. Asian actresses were primarily background fluff with few lines—the sidekick to the sidekick. I was one of these background characters. As I gained popularity on Myspace, I accepted an offer from an agent to rep me. He submitted me to the movie's casting department, and my significant presence in the import scene helped seal the deal. I had finally one-upped Tiara, who was also pursuing acting, snagging this role over her. As a result, I have the tiniest cameo in 2006's *The Fast and the Furious: Tokyo Drift*, the third installment of the series. In the short scene, I'm crowned in a baby-blue cowboy hat, wearing Daisy Dukes and a Victoria's Secret pushup bra underneath a scrap of a pink top. I stand beside two growling hunks of metal: a graphite Nissan 350Z and a navy-blue Nissan Silvia with an orange bumper. Boyishly handsome actor Satoshi Tsumabuki—who I was crushing on—strolls between the cars, drops his lit cigarette to the ground, and points at me. Nervously excited, I squeak, "Ready," as confidently as possible. Then he points across the way at another woman, my import bestie, popular Japanese import model Aiko Tanaka who says, "Seto." Tsumabuki belts, "Go!" and the cars take off, wheels squealing as they race into narrow parking lot tunnels.

Several years ago, the Thai American model Chrissy Teigen, who also had a brief cameo, tweeted, "My boobs are in fast and the furious Tokyo drift." She shared a clip of the scene captioned with the joke, "Make sure to not get her face." My boobs and face also made it into *Tokyo Drift* for about ten seconds, and I considered it a major achievement.

I enjoyed the film and only recently examined the movie critically. It's revealing that stunning future *Sports Illustrated* cover model Chrissy Teigen could be used as background fodder. Teigen, Aiko, and I were only three of the hundreds of Asian women used as background scenery in *Tokyo Drift*. Although the movie takes place in Japan, Asians were on the sidelines, and Asian women in particular appeared as the same objectified props as in every other Hollywood movie. I didn't consider these implications at the time; I was so excited to be part of a major movie production, especially one that became a beloved cult favorite. The cameo boosted my career, and for the next couple of years, Aiko and I were frequently hired to make appearances together at nightclubs and car shows as the girls from *Tokyo Drift*.

In the aftermath of Fast & Furious's explosive success, import car culture transformed from a tight-knit subculture created by Asian Americans into a mainstream spectacle for any man chasing fast cars and hot girls. What was once a niche community was suddenly flooded with young Asian American models, their hypersexualized images serving as endless digital fodder for fetishists to beat off to. Another unexpected consequence was the avalanche of non-Asian attendees and models, diluting the scene's original appeal. What was once a safe space for Asians and a venue for celebrating Asian identity lost its core, and Asian attendees stopped showing up. The scene faded, but not before birthing a new generation of Asian pinup girls now thriving on platforms such as Instagram and eventually OnlyFans. Instead of attending car shows, in a few clicks, fetishists could now easily satiate themselves from the privacy of their homes.

Because of the newly ubiquitous content from social media, the competition for likes and clicks also increased and the constant need to compete started to wear me down. Five years or so into my import modeling career, I wanted out. Despite my *Fast &*

Furious cameo fame, Tiara still caused male heads to turn away from me at every event or photo shoot I booked. With her beautiful, fine-featured face and sumptuous C-cups, she scored all the magazine covers that passed me over too. I had a mere moment to enjoy the warm glow of the male gaze before she effortlessly surpassed my blip in the sun. Tiara's fame made me realize my position was highly tenuous, dependent as it was on mercurial male attention—I was always on shaky ground, constantly scrambling and strategizing for that next magazine cover or achievement.

The competition was inescapable. Tiara and I orbited the same car shows, photo shoots, and parties. We were cautiously friendly, but we were more like frenemies than friends. One night at a rave with mutual friends, Tiara surprised me with a compliment. "Hey, I saw your new cover. It looks gorgeous. Congratulations."

She was referencing my cover shoot for *House of Roses* magazine, a "lad mag" geared at a Black male audience. I loved my spread and was proud of that cover. During the shoot, I stood atop an apple box (a wooden box used in film production) wearing a lime-green gown, clutching the chest of the rapper Mystikal, famous for the radio earworms "Shake Ya Ass" and "Danger (Been So Long)."

For a moment, I allowed myself to bask in her compliment, beaming next to my boyfriend. But then, in front of the entire group, she added, "I was actually scheduled to shoot it, but I was booked out of town." The words landed like a slap, deflating any sense of pride. I gripped my boyfriend's hand tightly, forced a smile, and said nothing. It wasn't the last time Tiara backhanded me with words, and I felt the invisible wedge between us driven deeper as our unspoken competition simmered beneath our placid faces. I later asked the photographer of the shoot about Tiara's comment and he said it was a lie.

We import models were merely trinkets and pawns in this male-driven world thriving on female objectification. We weren't in control of our narratives; we were mere commodities. In the import scene, there were glaring gender inequalities, with young women's looks judged harshly under a microscope, yet we competed to create the sexiest content as fodder for male arousal.

When women are pitted against one another for scarce resources, they may resort to attacking each other in an attempt to grasp a shred of power. In the import world, resources were limited—there were only a handful of magazine covers, calendars, and car shows and only so many male fans. The stress and futility of the situation likely exacerbated tensions between Tiara and me, causing us to undermine each other. We played a zero-sum game, built of systemic inequalities, and there could only be a single woman on top. As young women, we perpetuated existing gender stereotypes of "mean girls" instead of intertwining seamlessly as a braid in solidarity.

Eventually, the constant judgment wore me down. After earning enough credits, I transferred from my community college to the University of California, Los Angeles, where I eventually graduated and earned my bachelor's degree. Elitist as it may seem, I started to feel above being a pinup model. I set out to prove I had more to offer than just my body.

NOT LUCY LIU

Almost every Asian woman growing up in the early aughts has been called Lucy Liu—the quintessential dragon lady of the decade—at one point. The stereotype that we all look alike permeates Western media, reducing us into a monolith. Usually, it's random men name-checking Lucy Liu as some lazy attempt at a pickup line, as if my entire identity could be encapsulated in that one name. But one time in particular, the man serving my frozen yogurt was certain I was the actress.

My favorite Pinkberry used to be located five minutes from my home until its devastating pandemic closure. That day, I treated myself to an afternoon snack after a busy morning of emails and computer work. I rolled up dressed in a loose T-shirt and gray sweats, my hair in a messy bun. The chirpy, tall blond at the counter took my order but gave me a funny look before he turned to use the frozen yogurt machine. He twirled back around with a big smile.

"You're Lucy Liu!" he exclaimed.

"I'm definitely not," I replied, and smiled as he topped my yogurt with Cap'n Crunch, raspberries, and mango.

"It's okay. I won't tell anyone," he said, winking as he handed me my order.

It's as if my own face didn't exist in his eyes, completely erased by a celebrity he couldn't separate my features from. Lucy may have a doppelgänger, but it's certainly not me, especially with my platinum-blond hair. We look nothing alike. Yet, like many Asian women I know, I've been called Lucy Liu more times than I can count. In the early aughts, it was practically slang for "Asian girl." She was one of the most significant and memorable Asian women on television in the 1990s because she was practically the only Asian woman on TV.

Liu's breakout role was as Ling Woo in the television drama *Ally McBeal*. The show centers around a young attorney working at a sexually charged but prestigious law firm. Liu initially tried out for another role, which eventually went to Portia de Rossi, but creator David E. Kelley was so impressed by her audition that he wrote Ling Woo—a mysterious, dominatrix-tinged character coated with dragon lady stereotypes—specifically for Lucy Liu. This stereotype originated in the 1930s in roles played by the Asian American movie star Anna May Wong. The term was often used to describe powerful and influential Asian female figures such as China's Madame Chiang Kai-shek (aka Soong Mei-ling), Vietnam's Madame Nhu (aka Tran Le Xuan), and the much-despised Yoko Ono, who was viciously villainized in popular media as the dragon lady and witch who broke up the Beatles,* according to Sheridan Prasso in *The Asian Mystique: Dragon Ladies, Geisha Girls, and Our Fantasies of the Exotic Orient.*

Dragon lady generally refers to a sexually voracious, conniving, powerful, and reptilian Asian female villain. I don't know Liu personally, but she doesn't convey these characteristics in interviews I've watched. She seems down-to-earth and hardly the villainous dominatrix. What about meeting Liu caused Kelley to craft a highly sexualized, generic dragon lady character written just for her? Was it something she actually said? Or did he instantly paint her with his preconditioned Asian female stereotypes?

To Kelley's credit, Liu's role stole scenes as one of the most electrifying, fun, and charismatic characters on the show. She's the first dragon lady seductress character that's burned into my mind. Upon first meeting Ling Woo on the show, Ally McBeal and another female lawyer from the firm describe her contemptuously, repeating what a white man said earlier, "that American men like slutty Asian women," and accusing her of dressing provocatively for men, even when Woo is primly dressed. McBeal's skirts are much shorter, and McBeal admits she specifically wears these miniskirts to attract male attention.

Woo is also painted as a heartless, emasculating seductress (al-

---

* This accusation is a complete distraction from John Lennon's known Asian fetish, his violence against women, and his serial philandering. He left Yoko Ono for a year and a half when he had an affair with his decades younger Chinese assistant, May Pang.

though later character development enriches her beyond the stereotype). She tells her boyfriend if they have sex, he'll go blind because the sex will be so mind-blowing, adding that once men sleep with her, they're obsessed and can't get enough. She also gives men "hair jobs" with her silky long black hair. Unlike other characters on the show, she gets a growling sound effect added when she sneers—just another nod to the dragon lady stereotype as "other" and animalistic.

Liu went on to play several iconic dragon lady–esque characters: another sexy dominatrix in the action movie *Payback* (1999), starring Mel Gibson, and the deadly cold-blooded assassin O-Ren Ishii in Quentin Tarantino's *Kill Bill: Vol. 1* (2003). Her career soared high above both Sung-Hi's and mine at a time when we were both making an effort to break into film. In 2000, she scored the role of Alex Munday, the sexy crime-fighting dominatrix in the director McG's film *Charlie's Angels*—a remake of the popular 1970s TV show. The candy-coated confection of a hit movie banked $125 million at the domestic box office. In one of her most iconic scenes, Liu is sheathed in a shiny, formfitting leather jacket and skirt. Red lipstick gleaming and flawless, she stands before a chalkboard and a classroom of men. Riding crop in hand, the men quiver and wince in pleasure as this dominatrix brand of sexuality inspires them into impassioned activity like a swarm of worker ants to the pulsating queen.

The movie is pure frothy entertainment. McG started his career as a music video director, and the film was full of glamorous action and eye-catching effects. Liu's Munday is sharply contrasted with the sweet hopeless romantic character played by Cameron Diaz and the playful but reckless Angel played by a redheaded

Drew Barrymore. Like Ling Woo, Alex Munday is all business, cold and calculating. Liu is still very much a dragon lady in *Charlie's Angels*, but a much softer and more palatable one than her character in *Ally McBeal*.

Liu has argued against critics, proudly proclaiming she helped further Asian American visibility in film. Many believe that she played into Asian stereotypes, but she maintains that her *Charlie's Angels* character normalized Asian women in everyday roles. Having pursued acting during that time, I can see both sides of the argument. While the rest of us resorted to playing strippers and ornamental background objects, Liu scored plum leading roles. Yes, she played into the dragon lady sex fantasy, but I don't see how she could have avoided it. I certainly would have accepted any of the roles she played without question. It was an impossible situation for Asian actresses, and she exceeded all expectations, doing a phenomenal job with what was available and ultimately breaking down huge barriers for Asian actresses.

———

Personally, the dragon lady was never my preferred trope; it reminded me too much of my domineering tiger mom. Though I had plenty of fun toying with men—withholding sex and acting dismissive—I was rarely domineering or emasculating. Perhaps that's why I didn't resonate with Lucy Liu or her characters. Although Liu was a huge pop culture influence and household name, she wasn't a role model like Sung-Hi Lee was for me. I admired Liu's work and success, but she rose to fame after my formative years, after college.

Besides, Liu's the type of Asian girl I could never relate to. I imagined her a wholesome, goodie-two-shoes type, the kind of high-achieving Asian girl staring down on the slutty version of Asian like me. Though she played sexually voracious roles, she seemed straight edged; in fact, she says she's never even tried a drug in her life! While I leaned into the sweet China doll aesthetic in my photos, I considered myself a rebel, unafraid to break down conventional boundaries. I was also an avid druggie, trying every substance I encountered.

Our only similarity is that when attempting to break into Hollywood, both our early roles were as topless strippers, begging the question of whether playing a sex worker is a rite of passage for Asian actresses. Liu has a scene as a topless stripper in *City of Industry* (1997). The performance was much racier than I expected, opening with Liu in a black latex bikini and leather thigh-high boots, sliding down a pole and crouching on the floor with her hand on her crotch. Then there's *Full Metal Jacket*, with actress Papillon Soo Soo playing a Vietnamese prostitute. She's clad in a loose hot-pink crop top and leather miniskirt, approaching American soldiers with the unfortunately iconic line "Me so horny, me love you long time," before offering a blow job in exchange for money. The soldiers ask what they get for ten dollars, and she replies, "Everyting you want." Another is Nancy Kwan as Suzie Wong in the 1960 movie *The World of Suzie Wong*. Based on the 1957 book by Richard Mason, the unintentionally ludicrous description for the book on Amazon reads: "the timeless story of the love affair between a British artist and a Chinese prostitute." (So, the quintessential love story between a white man and an Asian woman is that of a white man and an Asian sex worker?)

There's also *Miss Saigon*, one of the most popular Broadway plays, about a Vietnamese prostitute who falls in love with an American soldier.

The list goes on, ad infinitum.

When I pursued an acting career at the peak of my modeling popularity, I played a stripper in the film *Dark Blue* (2002), a feature film starring Kurt Russell. Pursuing acting was practically a necessary step for pinup models to gain respect, so I followed suit. Sung-Hi successfully transitioned into acting, booking small parts in movies and guest star roles on TV shows. Both Pamela Anderson and Jenny McCarthy both broke out into mainstream television. It seemed integral to advancing my career and appeared fun.

My first acting manager was Peter. He pushed me incessantly to audition for Cinemax movies—glorified pornos with a whisper of a storyline but without actual penetration. This type of movie was so common on Cinemax that they were known as Skinemax flicks. I vehemently refused. I didn't think starring in nude titty films would garner the respectability I wanted so badly. Finally, he succeeded in convincing me to audition for the stripper role in *Dark Blue*.

"You'll get your SAG card, and it pays the full day rate plus residuals!" he said excitedly. SAG cards are a prized score for new actors, hard to earn, so I acquiesced. It wasn't a Skinemax movie; it was a legitimate film, a real production, and would be a great résumé credit.

On shoot day, I meekly tiptoed onto set in a robe and clear Lucite stripper shoes. Although a closed set—industry-speak for only essential crew—at least twenty people still worked during my scene. This included fifteen crew members, mostly men, and five other Asian extras. I had zero experience pole dancing and was anxious from the first take. To my horror, as I rounded the pole, my foot slipped, and a stiletto flew across the room and thudded loudly to the floor. The room was silent.

"Oops, we lost one!" Kurt Russell joked, breaking the tension. Kurt, Scott Speedman, and the cast and crew were beyond respectful, eyes averted from my nakedness except when Kurt motioned toward me while in character. Nevertheless, it was humiliating as the sole naked person in a sea of clothed ones. No one remembered to hand me my robe between takes, and I was too timid to speak up, wrapping my arms awkwardly around my bare chest. Luckily, I was only topless, but even to this day, I'm too traumatized to ever shoot naked in a major production again. It was nothing like the intimate pinup shoots I was accustomed to.

After *Dark Blue*, I booked small speaking parts in independent films, but it was my last major production for years. I continued auditioning for various iterations of the Asian sex worker, with the stray Asian reporter or kung fu fighter thrown in. It was the bulk of what was available for Asian actresses then. Unlike me, Sung-Hi managed to book roles, many times as sex workers but also a couple of interesting parts, like a sexy lesbian fighter in the TV series *Mortal Kombat: Conquest*. I did not have that luxury.

Being an aspiring actress in Hollywood was a grind, but for Asian American actresses, the obstacles felt even more insurmountable. With a dearth of meaningful roles and the weight of systemic bias, the climb was precipitous. Casting agents often called you in for auditions the night before, so it was hard to hold a regular job. No-name actresses like me were treated like scum, and being an aspiring Asian actress meant we were interchangeable. I'm jealous of actors today who can record their auditions and email them in without ever leaving home. Before things went digital, we trudged from audition to audition, often across town, toting our black-and-white headshots with our résumés stapled to the back. This was before Waze, Google Maps, and smartphones. I'd print out multiple sets of directions on MapQuest, praying the instructions were correct because they were often wrong.

On a typical multiple audition day, I'd answer a casting call in the morning for a slutty hooker in Hollywood, with another scheduled just one hour later for a wholesome Asian girl in, say, a Walmart commercial that would be across town in Santa Monica. It's almost impossible to make it from Hollywood to Santa Monica in that time during rush hour. After fighting traffic on the I-10, I'd hopefully find parking that wasn't too far. Then I'd remove my prostitute makeup to change into another outfit in the back seat. If nearby parking wasn't available, I might hike over in high heels through the stifling, breeze-less Southern California heat from blocks away. Once reaching the casting office, I'd wait an hour to get called in—even though I was on time—and get just five to ten minutes to wow the jaded casting director.

The ideal setting would be private face time with the casting director, but often the audition room was filled with a sea of carbon copies—Asian actresses with the same hair, build, and faces. At one of these auditions, I stood in a lineup, wearing blue stiletto heels and a matching skintight tube dress. (I wore this standard bimbo uniform to most of my acting auditions, since the role was usually for a stripper, prostitute, or massage parlor girl.) The director, later accused by six women of sexual assault, walked up and down evaluating the line of exposed cleavages and thighs. Feeling instantly uncomfortable, I looked to the ground, avoiding eye contact as other women preened and smiled. I didn't get the part.

That casting call was for a role in the blockbuster *Rush Hour 2* (2001), starring Jackie Chan and Chris Tucker. In the memorable massage parlor scene—a hit with many men—Tucker and Chan watch expectantly as two mama-sans in pink silk qipao dramatically pull back screen doors to reveal a cavalcade of twenty-eight scantily dressed Asian women looking back at them flirtatiously. Import models Natasha Yi and Felicia Tang sit prominently in the middle as Tucker's character laughs in glee. "This place is off the hook!" he exclaims. He orders five women for service as if ordering off a fast-food menu, calling it a "buffet line."

Asian women in film and TV are often portrayed as a remedy for men's homesickness and exhaustion—tools to ease their discomfort. Like *Full Metal Jacket* and *Memoirs of a Geisha*, this scene normalizes prostitution as if it's a reflection of average, everyday women in Asia. Although there is certainly a sex tourism industry, developed largely to meet the demands created by war and occupation, it's hardly representative of most women in Asia and certainly not of Asian American women.

———

Acting for me was just a way to boost credibility. I loved being in front of a camera, but I found little joy in memorizing lines and building a character's backstory. It was too much constant rejection for something I didn't love. I eventually quit after slogging around Hollywood with no success, but not before auditioning for a major motion picture that ended up being one of the most expensive television series ever produced at the time.

At 3:14 a.m. on a Thursday, my agent emailed me: "NOTE: CALL UP YOUR ACTING COACH TO WORK ON THIS WITH YOU. THIS ROLE IS A GAMECHANGER. PLEASE DYE YOUR HAIR A NATURAL COLOR TO REFLECT THE PERIOD PIECE." I woke up suddenly at 4:00 a.m. as if anticipating this email and was surprised by my inbox. The audition was that day in Santa Monica at 3:30 p.m. *Seriously?* I thought. *Production couldn't give the actresses at least twenty-four hours to prepare for the audition?* It was ridiculous that I was expected to call my acting coach last minute and dye my hair all in the same day.

The audition was for a series regular, a main role on a brand-new prestige Netflix series called *Marco Polo*. I was not surprised to learn that white men created, produced, and directed the series. It would shoot for four months in Malaysia and had a ten-episode commitment. The description for the character was as follows:

[MEI LIN] (20s, CHINESE): A sexy vamp murderess. A famous beauty and Emperor's courtesan, she's highly trained in the sexual bedroom skills that have helped to elevate her family in the royal court. Her station is jeopardized when the emperor dies so she must use her sensual prowess to win over the new emperor—it's the mission of her life. NUDITY REQUIRED.

There were two scenes required for the audition, and I was especially concerned about the sex scene. It was just a handful of lines, but they were cloaked in cheesy imagery such as the dragon tattoo on her back and a jade ornament affixed in her bun, and stage directions comparing her to "liquid silk" as she rode the politician. Another direction described her ass, half-lit by candles, while she brought the governor to the edge of cardiac arrest during sex. The final description in the scene calls Mei Lin "the most dangerous fuck in all of China" and proceeds to describe her riding "the white tiger." After reading the sides, I thought, *How the fuck do I audition this? Do I have to mime the sexual acts?* I had auditioned for sexualized roles in the past, but not ones with such explicitly described movements. I frantically emailed my acting teacher, asking for a last-minute coaching before 2:00 p.m. There would be an extra charge for the last-minute scheduling.

I spent all morning memorizing four pages of lines, and fortunately my acting teacher, Sal Landi, was available to help. I'd been taking his class for about a year. Sal was a working character actor with a career spanning decades. "I feel like you have tremendous potential, combined with a great look. If you could just commit fully to the craft, I bet you could go far," he'd say. Even though I didn't enjoy the work of acting or attending class, Sal's classes were more enjoyable than others. His was a scene study class, and Sal gave me parts I could sink my teeth into that weren't cloaked in ethnicity or stereotypes. He encouraged pushing beyond my boundaries.

Sal arrived at my place at around noon, and we set to work. "You don't actually have to ride the casting director or anything like that, but you need to exude so much sexuality that the camera captures it and the casting directors feel it across the room." Using the sense memory technique, he had me close my eyes and visualize when I was most sexually aroused.

I closed my eyes, feeling extremely awkward. Sex back then was merely performative; I was rarely fully aroused. The best I could do was fantasize about evoking my own sensuality. I tried reading the lines with Sal, but the dialogue was so absurd, I could hardly speak the first sentence without bursting out in hysterics. In the stereotype-drenched line, Mei Lin compares the governor's penis to a white tiger and her vagina to a jade portal, and talks about the tiger entering the portal. By the end of the one-hour session, I could manage a phone operator type of sexiness and at least get through the scene without giggling.

After he left, I threw on a black wig I had from previous photo shoots. It looked obviously fake, but there was no way I was dying my hair. I squeezed into a tight little black dress and stiletto heels and rushed out the door to battle rush-hour traffic. I mean, really, *3:30 p.m. for an audition?* Getting there would be brutal, and it would take two hours to return home. Once I got into the casting office, I waited another hour before the casting director called me into the room. I was sweating under the heavy wig, thanks to the sweltering Southern California heat. The audition itself was so quick that it's a blur. The casting director was curt, reciting lines back to me in monotone. I didn't nail the audition, but I don't think I completely bombed it either. I was in and out in less than ten minutes.

Unfortunately, I didn't get a callback, and shortly after that audition, I quit acting entirely. I would have accepted the role if I'd booked it, but it was obvious from the call sheet that to succeed as an actress, even more nudity would be required. I'd posed for enough nudes for a lifetime and didn't have it in me anymore.

When *Marco Polo* was released in 2014, it was an overblown celebration of Asian exoticism. It's an orgy-filled production riddled with stereotypes and little depth. Naked concubines abound, and the starring female characters are frequently reduced to sex objects without serious character development. The actress who won the role of Mei Lin, Olivia Cheng, delivered a superb performance, but her scenes required even more nudity than expected. I would have been incredibly uncomfortable on set—even more so than on *Dark Blue*. The role required constant and unnecessary nakedness. There were numerous sex scenes with men and women and even a completely nude fight scene with flips, kicks, and turns. Compare Mei Lin's nude fight with a similarly sexualized character, Daenerys Targaryen in *Game of Thrones*. Daenerys is frequently nude, but only in situations where it made sense, like intercourse or her emergence from a fire, reborn. She is never battling men nude or riding a dragon naked. The fact that Mei Lin is kung fu fighting men nude is categorically gratuitous. In no way does it drive the story forward.

Like Liu's Ling Woo and Alex Munday, Mei Lin is a pure dragon lady—dangerous, mysterious, and deceptive; using her sexual prowess transactionally—except with relentless nudity and weaker writing. *The most dangerous fuck in all of China.*

The core of the dragon lady trope is that she is unknowable, alien, and menacing, furthering the stereotype of Asians as perpetual foreigners—a threat to Americans and their way of life. It's a product of systemic racism against Asian Americans, which played out as recently as during the COVID-19 pandemic, when we suffered racist attacks and slurs telling us to "go back to our country." According to Stop AAPI Hate, reported hate incidents targeted at AAPI women were 2.2 percent higher than attacks on men between March 2020 and March 2021.

Dragon ladies and the Asian strippers on television and in film are nothing more than exotic, foreign dominatrices. A certain class of men get off on the precariousness they embody. They may have more agency than the butterfly, geisha, and China doll, and perhaps they might even derive pleasure from their carnal instincts, but at the end of the day, they're still animalistic objects.

I was tired of being forced to play both with no options in between. I'm not Lucy Liu, and I didn't like acting enough to continue the grind until I landed my own Ling Woo–esque role.

"CANDY COATED SUGAR SEX"

Even though I made bold proclamations of pride, after just two years into modeling, I was unsettled. I hoped pursuing a music career would prove I had depth and substance—that I was more than some dumb naked internet model. I was sick of embodying fetishized and objectified fantasies, and unbeknownst to me, it was affecting my mental health.

In between modeling gigs, I tackled musical aspirations. I publicly announced my music pursuits and was invited to record two tracks for a 2002 compilation CD titled *Import Jams*. It was an independently produced one-off CD for fans of freestyle, a dance-pop electro-music style popularized by the Latino community in the late '80s. This genre was kept alive by Filipino American singers and groups in the Bay Area in the late '90s and early 2000s. Several notable freestyle artists appeared on the CD, such as One Vo1ce, M:G, and Natalise. The producer arranged studio sessions for me to record one original song, titled "More and More," and a cover of "Take My Breath Away."

Around the same time I was trying to break into music, Gwen Stefani launched her solo career with a quadruplet of silent dancing Asian girls tailing her—Love (Maya Chino), Angel (Jennifer Kita), Music (Rino Nakasone), and Baby (Mayuko Kitayama). They were known as the Harajuku Girls. Stefani received significant criticism; the music editor Hazel Cills, writing for *Vice*, called it a "fetishistic obsession with street girls from the Harajuku district of Tokyo, which is known for its Lolita-esque fashions." Mihi Ahn at *Salon* wrote that "Stefani has taken the idea of Japanese street fashion and turned these women into modern-day geisha," and "she's swallowed a subversive youth culture in Japan and barfed up another image of submissive giggling Asian women."

The Harajuku Girls, with their microskirts, heavy makeup, and knee-high socks, resembled the same Japanese schoolgirls and anime characters associated with Asian fetishes. (In my pin-up modeling days, the Japanese schoolgirl trope was one of my favorites; it worked like a charm to titillate men.) Even while the Harajuku Girls didn't act overtly sexual, they projected the same tired messaging that Asian women were mere enhancements, decorative props, or sex toys—like jewelry or a garter belt.

By contrast, the Bay Area Filipino freestyle and R&B acts—such as Jocelyn Enriquez, Buffy, Pinay, Innerlude, Kai, Devotion, Drop N Harmony, and Premiere, among others, who inspired my early tracks on *Import Jams*—sadly never went mainstream, and part of the reason could be how little they leaned into their Asianness. None of the female groups played into typical stereotypes the way the Harajuku Girls did.

Freestyle- and R&B-inspired Filipina girl groups and solo artists weren't highly sexed in imagery and song lyrics. Enriquez, one of the first Filipino Americans to sign a major label record deal, was more edgy than sexy. The music video for her top single, "A Little Bit of Ecstasy," focuses on futuristic dystopian imagery rather than her; she mainly appears in quick flashes or faraway shots. Ultimately, she charted on *Billboard* but never quite broke out. A similar thing happened when I attempted to break free from my fetishized image with my first single release, trying to cultivate a more refined, classy aesthetic instead. It was a flop.

My solo album debuted in 2003. I'd wanted to sing since elementary school, but Asian American singers didn't exist, so it seemed like a pipe dream. I had a platform to pursue this fantasy only after building my import fanbase and internet audience from scratch. Taking a huge leap from my sexualized pinup image, my first album was strangely cutesy. One of the lead singles was a love song more fit for high schoolers than adults called "Don't Say Goodbye," inspired by a favorite Britney Spears ballad, "From the Bottom of My Broken Heart." It was a saccharine breakup song with zero sexual undertones. Not surprisingly, the album didn't sell or attract the attention of record labels or media. More than one factor was likely at play, starting with the fact that the music wasn't great. But my audience was quite loyal and was undoubtedly confused by my new foray into music and the dialed-back sexualization.

As I licked my wounds from disappointing album sales, I fell deeper into the club and drug scene. I'll never forget my first hit of cocaine because I was instantly hooked.

"Want a bump?" my girlfriend Isabella said as a group of us clamored for mirror space in the VIP dressing room of a Hollywood club. Visionshock, an Asian American club promoter, had taken over for the night. The founders were my friends Eric Young and Billy Chen, and I was a weekly fixture at their events. There were multiple Los Angeles–based Asian promoters, each producing two or more parties weekly. The events were so popular it wasn't rare to get shut down by fire marshals, as promoters frequently packed clubs over capacity.

The Asian American clubbing and nightlife scene of the early 2000s was thriving in major cities like Los Angeles, San Francisco, New York, Seattle, Houston, and more. One of my favorite haunts was Le Privé, a Korean club on Western Avenue in Koreatown, well known for implementing the South Korean nightclub phenomenon of "booking," meaning waiters grabbed women off the club floor to meet single men who were sardined into expensive booths. The men wore head-to-toe black, had heavily gelled hair, and doused themselves in colognes such as Cool Water, Issey Miyake, and Eternity. Crown Royal shots were used as bait. We loved the exclusivity of Korean clubs; you couldn't just saunter in off the street. You needed to know a waiter, and groups of women got tables for free. The waiters had nicknames like Boxer, Superman, and Ninja. My waiter said Nicolas Cage came regularly, scouting for young Asian flesh. It was rumored that he met his first Asian wife there.

"I don't put anything up my nose," my friend Jessica sniffed as my ears perked up. After trying ecstasy and weed and graduating to Vicodin and Xanax, I was down for anything promising to knock me out of my head.

"I got plenty for everyone!" said Isabella, as she pulled out a sleek one-inch bullet filled with finely ground cocaine powder.

That first bump of cocaine rushed straight to my brain. Blanketed in a cloud of euphoria, I felt instantly confident, silky, and powerful. The ritual of cocaine seemed glamorous. I started smoking Parliaments for the cigarette filter's slight recession, the perfect fit for a coke bump. With my braided black Chanel watch around my wrist, I made a show of dipping the cigarette end into the stamp-size plastic baggie with my French manicured fingers. I felt fancy, like a jaded heiress with undeserved privilege.

I loved the cliquish, cocaine-fueled, in-crowd forays to the bathroom, sausaged into stalls in groups of three or more. We'd conscientiously check one another's noses afterward for leftover white residue. Even better were the club promoter's after-parties, with intimate cigarette-smoking groups perched around a glass table. While we waited expectantly, a ringleader crushed a delicate cocaine rock into pieces and eventually fine powder. The credit card chopped—*tap tap tap*—as my heart beat loudly in my eardrums, seeming to match the staccato of anticipation. The shared dollar bill siphoning the bitterness up my nostril was the instant funnel to obliteration. Even more than ritual, cocaine erased my trauma, shame, and the psychological stress humming so constantly I didn't realize it existed. Outwardly, as if to convince myself, I announced I didn't care what anyone thought of my life choices. The drugs seemed innocuous; in my mid-twenties, all my friends were partying, and I felt everything was under control. It was easy to restrict drug use to the weekends.

But soon, controlled partying leaked from weekends into weekdays. I balanced a nebulous cocktail of prescription drugs, trying to maintain the ideal high, on top of illegal substances. Our dealer's cocaine was low grade, laced with cheaper drugs. As a result, after a bump, I might feel instantly agitated instead of elated. I never again experienced the pure euphoria of that first time but compulsively chased the promise of it until sunlight streamed through my blinds. I carried a combination of pills—Xanax, Valium, and Ambien—to offset anxiety and ensure sleep at night's end.

One night, upon leaving my friend's house around 3:00 a.m., he asked, "Want a bump for the road?"

"Of course," I said, relieved to extend my high as he cut up a fat line of white powder.

"We're out of coke, though; all I have left is K," he said.

My heart dropped. I was heading home with my roommate, who was finished for the night, and didn't want to be high on a brand-new drug alone. But it was just a moment of uncertainty before deciding, *Fuck it,* and snorting the new substance. It felt nothing like cocaine, the burning and numbness. My momentary hesitation was unfounded; there was no need to be with anyone else on ketamine, also known colloquially as horse tranquilizer (it's an anesthetic used on humans and animals).

That night, I learned I didn't want euphoria, I wanted annihilation. I wanted to abandon my body, escaping my physicality. I have no memory of getting home but remember spending the night alone in a bedridden K-hole. Some find it terrifying; it's like an out-of-body experience. The feeling is hard to describe, like entering another dimension and watching your life upside down through a fish-eye lens while flying, and nothing makes sense. I couldn't move or talk but enjoyed separation from my body and life. The ketamine temporarily knocked loose the rattling thoughts in my head, preventing shame from taking root. There was an elegiac relief to realizing that nothing mattered, that my life made no sense. I had achieved internet fame for doing nothing more than posting photos viewed on a computer screen; I had gained renown for nothing. Although cocaine wiped away my emotions, ketamine ensconced me in complete detachment—my happy place. It was like applying the piano's soft damper pedal to life, evening out the sharp edges. Unfortunately, the dissociative effect left as soon as it wore off.

A couple years after my album tanked, I was no longer a high-functioning addict; it wasn't rare for me to blow off flights and appearances. My reputation as an unreliable model and performer grew, but I didn't care. Around this time, I stopped shooting nudes but still worked as a bikini and lingerie pinup. My modeling career and club and car show appearances worldwide funded my musical aspirations. Asian American nightclubs hired me to sing at parties for name recognition, not because my music was good. But often I was a no-show.

In the meantime, Gwen Stefani and her background lineup of obedient Japanese schoolgirls continued to tour the world, garnering cash and prizes, like performing at the MTV Video Music Awards. Even though they were nothing more than Stefani's giggling and preening accessories (it's rumored they were contractually not allowed to speak), they were showered with attention and recognition. In a *Rolling Stone* feature, Stefani said that she wanted them to "stand behind her and look cute" and "follow her everywhere." While my music career floundered, their popularity soared.

I watched excitedly (because I loved to see any Asian "representation" in music) and at the same time jealously, as the Harajuku Girls danced on the most enviable world stages. I would have done anything to be seen the way they were. But I refused to be background fodder for any artist.

———

After the music producer of Embryo Productions wrote me a song unabashedly about sex, my music career finally took off. The song, "Candy Coated Sugar Sex," premiered on Myspace in 2005.

Myspace was the first global social media site, revolutionary for its music-friendly interface, allowing artists to upload music easily. Myspace Tom—or Tom Anderson, one of the founders and the main face of the social media platform—personally invited me to join his social media platform. It was 2003, and Friendster went viral without the ability to handle the traffic, so its solution was to deactivate its most popular accounts. Tom reached out to the rejects like me and Tila Nguyen (who later rebranded herself as Tila Tequila) and invited us to join Myspace, "a place for friends." I was furious about my sudden Friendster account removal. I loved the yearbook/slam book style pages featuring countless "testimonials" from friends and fans. So, I accepted Tom's invite, partially in retaliation against Friendster for kicking me off. I had plenty of traffic from my personal website and a hefty email list I could redirect.

Within a few years of building my Myspace account, I grew a friend list of more than three hundred thousand followers—significant back then. Myspace allowed my music to gain fans beyond the Asian American import community. I reached audiences I would never have had access to, but only if I relied on old stereotypes and played the game.

It was later rumored that Myspace Tom had an Asian thing, so there may have been more to the invite than an innocent bid to grow his new social media platform. At this point, I was well aware of yellow fever; many of my followers, fans, and website subscribers were Asiaphiles. The opportunity came at an opportune time. Even if these invites came from a desire to bring various Asian women under the creator's orbit, Myspace helped Asian women gain visibility in the media. Yes, we still played to stereotypes of sexy China dolls and dragon ladies, but we felt somewhat in control of the narrative. I wouldn't have had a music career without Myspace.

The switch to Myspace proved especially fruitful in October 2006, after *Rolling Stone* included a section titled "The Girls of Myspace." There was a two-page feature on Tila Tequila, who had also launched a music career, and a blurb about three other female musicians, including me. It's significant there were two Asians out of the six ladies featured—Tila and me. "Like Tila Tequila, roller-skate-wearing Kaila oozes sex," reads the article—a reference to my "Candy Coated Sugar Sex" music video. By comparison, the profile of the white singer Colbie Caillat, right next to mine, describes her most downloaded tune, "Bubbly," as "a soulful acoustic number that wouldn't sound out of place on a Norah Jones record." It's an interesting contrast. Caillat, as a white woman, didn't need to rely on sex appeal to pursue an entertainment career. She could simply be wholesome and bubbly. Yet when I acted similarly in my debut album, it got zero traction.

"Candy Coated Sugar Sex" quickly charted millions of plays on Myspace, and I was soon one of the social media site's top ten female music artists. Embryo did not have an Asian fetish, although he was white. He mostly worked with rappers. The song he wrote for me was based on the fetishized imagery I posted myself on Myspace. His eroticized lyrics seemed an obvious fit for what I was promoting, hypersexualization, which was compounded even further in the music video.

The video was produced by an up-and-coming music director, Evan Jackson Leong, introduced to me by my then manager. The song starts with a '70s-style porn groove beat and synth intro—think the soundtrack to Quentin Tarantino's *Death Proof.* In the video, I cycle through a series of sexual, tropey, pop culture–infused outfits. To start, I'm dressed in some semblance of a cowgirl costume (alluding to my scene in *Tokyo Drift*), followed by my favorite, a schoolgirl getup nodding to the Harajuku Girls. My pink plaid miniskirt is combined with white thigh-high stockings and handcuffs affixed to the side of my skirt, as I sing with as much carnality as I can muster. Another outfit is a bright green jumper paired with boys' soccer knee socks and roller skates, invoking Rollergirl, the porn star character from the movie *Boogie Nights* (the outfit referenced in *Rolling Stone*). The video even included shots of my body parts and face tinted green to give the impression of night vision footage, mimicking Paris Hilton's blurry 2004 leaked sex tape (filmed when she was just nineteen; she alleged her decade older boyfriend coerced her into shooting it). Although the resulting video sucked, the song was such a success on Myspace that MTV Chi, a spin-off network launched in 2005 targeting Chinese Americans, aired the video and asked me to perform the song at a live show.

The performance was the biggest show of my life. MTV Chi focused on Asian American pop culture and music, and this event promoting its recent launch featured the hottest names in Asian American music, including MC Jin, Burning Tree Project, Far East Movement, Jeff and Machi, and me. It was an honor to be included, as I was often shunned from performing at mainstream Asian American events like Kollaboration and the Unforgettable Gala. I assumed they thought I was too trashy as a former import model to be included in their high-caliber events. But MTV did not discriminate.

As I stood behind the curtain, waiting for my cue, wearing only a robe over my minuscule purple chain-metal dress, the host shouted, "MTV, put your hands together for Kaila Yu!" The crowd cheered for the band finishing onstage—Frequency 5, a pop-punk band led by Johnny Lee—and I threw off my robe, marching confidently onstage. I was not a dancer, but I had rehearsed my first song, "Move," for months and shook my hips, confidently wiggling alongside my choreographer with four female backup dancers. Wearing skintight black dresses, they expertly performed the more advanced dance moves I couldn't master.

After the four-minute routine, the following number was "Candy Coated Sugar Sex." It was my most elaborate stage performance. I ran offstage, lifting my dress over my head, going through the practiced motions of our thoroughly rehearsed outfit change. We had forty-five seconds. One assistant held a towel to shield me while another squeezed me into my tiny black vinyl miniskirt, bra top, and thigh-high boots, which I wore underneath a virginal white nightgown gliding down to the floor.

I jumped onto the twin-size red silk-swathed bed purchased for this occasion. Four men each grabbed a corner of the bed frame and carried the bed and me to center stage. After plopping it down, all except one of the men quickly exited stage left. The one stagehand lingered, meandering slowly offstage, clad unassumingly in a white shirt and loose jeans. I leaped off the bed and grabbed him by his shirt, wheeled him around, unbuttoned his jeans, and quickly slipped them down as he ripped off his shirt in one motion. He was wearing only black briefs at this point. The crowd screamed in shock and glee, not expecting the mayhem at a family-friendly performance. ("You need to shock the crowd as Madonna would," my performance coach, Victor, said.) My performance partner sat on the bed facing the crowd, his jeans around his ankles, as I stood in front of him while he removed my nightgown to reveal the tiny black latex number underneath. I cooed:

> I know what the boys want, boys want, boys want
> I know what the girls like, girls like girls like
> I know what the boys want, boys want, boys want
> I know what the girls like, candy coated sugar sexxxxxxxxy

My four backup dancers pranced back onstage and gyrated to the right of the bed. Continuing to sing, I lay atop my partner, and he pulled me across his body—skin on skin. I flipped to my back, swiveling my hips up and down on his. Two dancers marched to either side of the bed, one pulling her leg into a standing split while the other grinded her hips on the floor, her head tossed back and hair spilling over her body. I continued to sing, whispering the lyrics and harmonizing over a throbbing club beat:

> You probably look at me and think that I'm innocent
> But I get this feeling and I wanna get into it
> I know you like my sugar, I like your cinnamon

The song is a dance anthem that played seamlessly into the butterfly trope, a continuation of the message I conveyed as a pinup model: docile and compliant, yet hypersexual. With seductive lyrics and the suggestive performance, I was once again proclaiming myself as a willing sex doll, ready to fulfill the whims of men. It was empowering to command the stage and feel in control of the sensual image I created, but I hated that it felt like this stereotype was my only path to success. In my teens, I was a fan of Coco Lee, a Chinese American singer known as the "Mariah Carey of Taiwan." I watched as she tried to achieve her ultimate dream—mainstream fame in the United States. One of her singles, "Do You Want My Love," charted a bit in December 1999. I remember cringing when watching the music video, which opened with a rapper repeatedly saying, "Uh-oh, Coco." The video was a watered-down version of Jennifer Lopez's music video for "If You Had My Love"—the lead single off her musical debut, released in May 1999—but with none of the sexiness. In Lee's music video, she's wholesome as she mugs and grins at the camera while singing lyrics such as "Do you want my love? Can you make me sweat? Do you want it bad enough to make it soaking wet." It was totally incongruent. Coco Lee didn't embrace the hypersexual Asian route and it seemed like it hurt her debut, the same way my heartfelt ballad tanked from the start.

It's arguable that in the hypersexual landscape of the 2000s, I just acted like a typical pop star. The stark difference was that white pop stars had more narrative autonomy and didn't have to navigate the intersection of fetishization and objectification. While plenty of white and Black pop stars were hypersexualized, there were other, less objectified performers showcasing a wider gamut of femininity like Alanis Morissette, Erykah Badu, Lauryn Hill, Colbie Caillat, and Pink. Asian women were particularly boxed in. White men directed our media narratives, and only within this recognized framework could we find mainstream success. I believed there was no demand for me as a wholesome singer-songwriter with a guitar; I felt required to sell sex. My instant success after "Candy Coated Sugar Sex" was no exception. It was proof.

The problem? Sexualizing myself and feeding into the butterfly trope came with a significant mental toll. Playing the insatiable Asian pinup chick was exhausting and inauthentic. I constantly wore a fabricated persona. I was intoxicated by the attention, but performing sexiness to a live audience to receive said adulation felt like an impossible task. I could easily contort my body and play the part of a coy geisha with a still camera, but in front of thousands of people, I couldn't sustain this false sex appeal for extended periods.

For me, hypersexualization was a form of emotional violence and dehumanization, an unconscious version of self-objectification and fetishization. It was a rejection of my true self and a defiant act of self-hate, albeit unknowingly. Below a layer of consciousness, my assault video taunted me with the irony of performing the tropes that first led me to assault. It's the result of years of internalized racism, manifesting from a subconscious belief of inherent inferiority. I felt I needed to fetishize myself to have value. None of it came naturally, and I slowly annihilated everything authentically me.

My website videographer once said, "You don't know how to be sexy. You happen to be naked, young, and hot, so you just have to exist to turn a guy on. In real life, you're a shy bookworm." He encouraged me to be more like Reese, a smoldering Italian Playmate he worked with. She exuded sex effortlessly, on and off camera. After a shoot, we went for coffee, and I stood next to Reese as she ordered. She said nothing out of the ordinary, but as I watched, she smiled suggestively at the barista, biting her lip, and looking him up and down like he was a tasty treat. As a result, our order was on the house.

As we sipped our coffees, Reese shared she'd go to expensive restaurants with a girlfriend, decked out in slinky dresses and stiletto heels. They rarely paid for meals, seductively eyeing men at nearby tables, inevitably enticing one to join and to foot the bill. Sexiness oozed from Reese's pores. In contrast, my sexiness was a facade. I could never stroll into a restaurant like Reese and charm my way into a free meal. Even now, I'm an unskilled flirt. I could perform sexuality, but it was inauthentic. I could wiggle my hips suggestively, but I was no dancer. Without my circus act of four dancers and a shirtless ripped model, my performances felt anticlimactic, dull, and uninspired. My hypersexual image was a mirage. The eyeballs trained on me gave validation and a rush of pleasure, but the upkeep was as exhausting as it was diametrically opposed to my true self.

To overcome my shortcomings as a sex symbol, I doubled down on drugs, allowing the high to obliterate my insecurities and fears. Drugs were an instant boon for my introversion, transforming me into a doe-eyed vixen without a care in the world.

After returning home from the MTV performance and a subsequent mini tour in Germany performing a pared-down version of my MTV stage show (without backup dancers), my producer, Embryo, wrote several new songs for my new album. We gathered weekly at an Inglewood recording studio. I always arrived high or recovering from an all-nighter; the combined nasal drip from snorting K or coke and hoarseness from smoking copious Newports made the vocals we recorded unusable. We never finished any of the new songs.

I went on a bender for the next year. My sporadic cocktail of cocaine, K, Ambien, and Xanax led to blackouts, hallucinations, and highly erratic behavior, which I rarely remembered. There was one time I thought my roommate, Kevin, had barged into my studio recording session. When he snapped at me, I awoke from my drug-addled haze and realized I was crouched on my knees in my bedroom, singing into an imaginary microphone. I hadn't been to the studio in months.

Everything I had built turned to dust.

SLANTED

The first time I saw my vagina was with the rest of the world.

I'd never looked at my girl parts before my assault video. After all, it's not easy to get a good look at your labia; you must either sprawl out with a hand mirror or spider your legs into an uncomfortable, unflattering manner to take it all in.

I had no interest in watching my recorded assault, but I viewed a few clips with averted eyes, needing to know what millions had already seen. In the video, I'm mostly hidden by pubic hair. At nineteen, I was a virgin and had no plans for anyone to see my private parts that day or anytime soon. In fact, up until that video, I never even thought about that part of myself.

To start, we never talked about sex at home, and I've never seen my parents touch. The thought that they ever had sex for anything more than functional pregnancy was more than I could stomach. My first awareness of my sexuality was in seventh grade at Upland Junior High. I was eating a dry hamburger with other honors students when Juan, a handsome but weaselly kid with slicked-back hair and wearing a white T-shirt, shorts, and knee socks, sidled up, snaking his arm around my waist.

"You're so beautiful," he whispered in my ear. "I heard it's slanted."

I was confused and wondered if *slanted* was a sexual term I'd never heard of. His attention made me feel embarrassed, flattered, and even somewhat turned on. Normally, I was invisible. However, I knew from his lecherous tone that what he had said was bad. Soon after, I learned he would approach the nerdiest and ugliest junior high girls only to mumble obscene comments in their ears. After a classmate explained "slanted vaginas" was a racist insult, I became deeply insecure that boys thought I had a deformed or sideways vagina.

The myth of Asian women's "horizontal" rather than "vertical" vaginas has been in the zeitgeist since the 1850s, when Chinese women were sold into sex slavery in San Francisco during the California gold rush, according to Judy Yung in *Unbound Voices: A Documentary History of Chinese Women in San Francisco*. Although the rumor infects all Asian women, it was first directed at the Chinese. It's hard to know where this myth originated, but sources suggest it persisted since Chinese Americans were segregated from the general public. Then in the nineteenth century, when Asians became the "yellow peril," painted as rats swarming American shores to steal jobs, this rumor rocketed back into the atmosphere. Later, during U.S. military occupations in Asia, soldiers kept the falsehood alive as a joke.

Chinese men were painted as disgusting and despicable creatures, while all Chinese women were perceived as filthy, diseased prostitutes with deformed sex parts. When male Asian laborers first immigrated to the United States, most couldn't afford to bring wives. However, between 1852 and 1873, approximately 87 percent of Chinese women immigrants were trafficked by the Chinese secret society Hip Yee Tong for forced marriage or prostitution. Tong organizations often bribed local authorities to smuggle the women in. Then in 1854, the U.S. government enacted a series of laws against Chinese "prostitutes." Later, the Page Act of 1875 targeted immigrants from "China, Japan, or any Oriental country," barring their entry if they arrived for "lewd and immoral purposes," painting a scarlet letter onto Asian women in the public record. A Republican California congressman, Horace F. Page, sponsored the bill, wanting to "send the brazen harlot who openly flaunts her wickedness in the faces of our wives and daughters back to her native country." Senator Cornelius Cole concurred, calling Chinese women "the most undesirable of population, who spread disease and moral death among our white population."

In 1876, J. Marion Sims, the respected president of the American Medical Association, claimed, with no factual basis, that Chinese prostitutes passed syphilis to white boys as young as eight years old. Dr. Hugh H. Toland testified that "Chinese prostitutes were spreading a unique strain of syphilis that failed to respond to therapy and proved deadly for his white patients," according to Columbia University professor Jennifer Lee, writing for the Brookings Institution. Even though white prostitutes far outnumbered the Chinese, these "experts" falsely argued that only beastly Chinese prostitutes stooped to servicing underage boys.

By 1890, the ratio was one Chinese woman for every twenty-seven Chinese men. To call these women prostitutes is beyond euphemism, as many were slaves. Some were kidnapped, but poverty-stricken Chinese families also sold daughters into slavery. Once arriving on American shores, victims were often held in barracoons, the same enclosures used for enslaved Africans. These "prostitutes" were sometimes openly auctioned off and sold before large crowds.

The living conditions in California brothels, mainly in Los Angeles and San Francisco, were shocking. Living quarters were known as "cribs" for their tiny size. These women received no medical care, inevitably contracting venereal diseases, and "most women were broken within a few years," writes Lynne Yuan for HistoryNet.com. According to the San Francisco historian Gary Kamiya, in an article for the *San Francisco Chronicle*, many died after five or six years of slavery, sometimes sentenced to death by mandate if they were too sick to perform. Often prostitutes were tossed out onto the street to die.

Newspapers, government documents, and respected medical books and journals published this "evidence" of diseased and nymphomaniac Chinese women for the public record. But the hypersexual Asian trope is rooted in the anguish of mostly sex-trafficked Chinese prostitutes. This trope painted victims, forced to have sex against their will—the mirror opposite of hypersexual—as insatiable, deformed, and unclean. Like a rapacious flea, this trope hopped from Chinese victims and carried over to all Asian women—and is still sucking the dignity out of Asian women today.

The other, more modern belief that persists is that Asian

women have tighter vaginas. Like the "slanted" rumor, the origins of this misconception are unknown, but most suspect it's rooted in colonialism, World War II, the Korean War, and the Vietnam War, when thousands of Asian women were coerced and trafficked into prostitution with white American soldiers. Military bases were surrounded by prostitution rings offering sexual services to otherwise homesick American soldiers. As a result, Western civilization's first major encounter with Asian women was in the context of sexual domination and military conquest.

Asian women are often smaller and daintier than their Western counterparts, and perhaps within the context of sexual domination, the rumor spread they were tighter because of their smaller stature. Additionally, there's an inherent infantilization with the "tighter" myth, as it also assumes virginity. Although the slanted genitalia belief has fallen by the wayside, this belief persists. Some of the most common comments on my fan sites were about my vagina, how it was extra tight (and slanted). Phrases like "Sucky sucky" and "Fucky fucky" were daily occurrences. And often men would describe wanting to eat my p#ssy fried rice or p#ssy chow mein.

The handful of white men I've slept with have all commented on my tightness and the overall tininess of my body parts and frame. They also commend my soft and silky skin (something many Asian women hear). It's almost as if Asian women are a different species. These comments make me feel precious, cherished, and doll-like, but also like an object to be dissected and cataloged by parts. Concurrently, there's a disquieting feeling of being a faceless assemblage of parts to be dichotomized, collected, and itemized. Instead of a whole person, I'm fragmented into skin to be stroked, hair to pulled, and a pussy to be fucked. I enjoy the fleeting validation, but there's the underlying knowledge that I'm being stripped of personhood, dehumanized, and invalidated. Notably, not a single Asian man I have slept with has ever commented on my body size or skin in that way.

———

Because of my pinup model past, sex was always performative. I needed to look perfect and have optimal lighting during sex. Candlelight was ideal, neon light was a no, and bright, fluorescent light was a hell no. My lover became a stand-in for the camera I was always posing for; I knew my best angles, how to arch my back just so, and the most flattering leg positions. Without curated lighting and choreography, my stretch marks, cellulite, and imperfections were exposed for scrutiny. The intimacy and vulnerability required for real sex was terrifying, stripping me of the control I had mastered in front of the lens.

In my personal life, I was hardly like the hypersexual Asian trope. I didn't lose my virginity until my sophomore year of college and didn't find sex particularly enjoyable for years, pretending to enjoy it as a service to my first boyfriend. To be pleasing, I even purchased books about becoming a better lover, but by the end of that four-year relationship, after the puppy love had faded, sex was a chore, and I just lay there waiting for him to get it over with.

Over the years, I slowly developed more vulnerability and experienced orgasms, but the man's pleasure still reigned supreme. My gratification was intrinsically tied to his; the more excited and pleasured he was by me, the more I'd be turned on. For me, sex has often been a mirage of true sexual satisfaction. I enjoy it— foreplay is great—but I've been able to orgasm during intercourse with only one man, which seems to be missing the point entirely. How many men would engage in sex if there was no release? My own sexual desires were like an indecipherable language I never learned. As someone who embraced fetishization, it was hard for me to fathom the concept of my own pleasure, separate and distinct from my lover's. I felt like I needed to live up to the manufactured sex symbol image I'd created every time. But that's impossible.

It would certainly help my satisfaction if I enjoyed receiving oral sex, but I'm not a fan. Maybe because my first experience receiving oral was during an assault for millions to see. That predator was the first person to see and touch me there besides a doctor. After that, countless viewers glimpsed me on a computer screen even before I had seen myself. I've blocked that experience and don't care to relive it, but even today, I'm not completely healed. I'll never be 100 percent. Combined with dissociation—that it feels like it happened to someone else (Elaine, not Kaila)—I don't believe I will fully experience the complete depth of vaginal pleasure until I come to terms with that first torture, which remains safely tucked behind badly scarred walls, compartmentalized into a silo as shoddily built as toddler-erected Lego sets. That predator wrenched away something priceless; I'll never know what receiving oral sex would have felt like before his violation. That act and my vagina will forever be linked to violence and the ensuing humiliation. Shame is the killer of pleasure.

Ever since my public assault, I'd hated my vagina. It's as if I blamed it for attracting bodily harm, instead of the unchecked, entitled, and celebrated enormity of male desire. My hate turned inward. Watching the video the first time, I became obsessed with my vagina's appearance. I wondered if I'd hate myself less if it were flawless. If it was, maybe I could erase the assault. As previous surgeries had made me feel reborn, I thought going under the knife again could be a new beginning. Besides, combined with the mythology and stereotypes around Asian vaginas, mine had to be nothing short of perfection. I fantasized about pulling down my labia and slicing them completely off with a quick snip of the scissors—such an easy fix.

So, ten years after the assault, I had them sliced off.

My gynecologist was a kindly Russian gentleman in his sixties I'd been going to for years. I learned he performed labiaplasty, a cosmetic procedure reducing the lips of the labia minora, so I went with him. I didn't research the quality of his work or shop around. I just wanted it done.

"Just take it all off," I told him. I didn't tell anyone about the procedure except my best friend, who gave me a ride home from the hospital. Afterward, I don't remember much, recovering in a haze of Percocet and bedridden for a week.

What I'll never forget is going to work a week later. I was a producer at an event company, and it was our yearly training. Since it was only two days of sitting, I figured I would be fine, packing extra Percocets. After eight hours of sitting upright in a hard chair, I was in excruciating pain because I should've been lying down. The extra pills I popped didn't help, and there was much more blood on my bandages. While carpooling with a co-worker back from Orange County, traffic took over two hours. I was thankful for the leather seats, as I could feel blood gushing out of my wound. Luckily, my thick bandages caught everything, but I prayed to get home immediately. Later my doctor told me I probably had a hematoma, a pooling of burst blood. It was fine, but I had to cancel the rest of my schedule to recover.

———

As I ruminate on my labiaplasty today, I'm troubled. Why did I feel compelled to slice up a body part probably only one or two more men would ever see in my life? Could it be some form of body dysmorphia? There's research linking emotional and sexual abuse to body dysmorphia as a trauma response. I absolutely developed a disdain for my vagina that didn't exist previously because of the horrifying, visceral experience with my assailant. I'm unequivocally certain that if I was never assaulted and forced to view my degradation and humiliation on camera, I wouldn't have undergone labiaplasty. My body dysmorphia was like a fun-house mirror. It was also a puzzle that could never be solved: I was trying to erase the assault, but how much of my disgust was rooted in internalized racism? Asian vaginas were supposed to be perfect, to appear untouched, to be pure and superior. As an Asian woman and a sex symbol, my vagina needed to embody that. I felt as though my assault tainted it, and I needed a totally new one to feel complete and whole again, as if cutting into it and crafting a new vagina would return my body to the virginal, pure, and perfect state that an Asian vagina needed to be. There's so much mythology and sexual lore around the Asian vagina, and without surgery, mine could never satisfy the myth.

But even after the surgery, I wasn't satisfied. I don't regret the surgery but wish I had shown my doctor a sample photo of what I wanted, because it didn't look perfectly flawless. Labiaplasty is a popular surgery for enhancing sexual pleasure or easing discomfort while wearing restrictive clothing. The purpose of mine was solely aesthetic; I would practically sacrifice all sexual satisfaction to have the world's most beautiful vagina. I want to believe if my doctor fashioned the perfect labia, I would happily invite men to go down on me, perhaps even orgasm easily and enjoy sex exponentially. The truth is, I'm uncertain I would ever be satisfied. Even if my doctor crafted perfection, my vagina's existence was a reminder of my assault. I want to be like Barbie, who has no vagina. That would be the only way to completely erase the violation.

I've always rationalized going under the knife was for me, but it's not entirely true. None of these decisions involved my own pleasure. Media and pop culture convinced me that fetishization was the key to validation. So, I sacrificed everything to achieve that ideal. My kowtowing to the performance of Asian fetish kept me distant from my sexual desire. My self-worth hinged on my ability to satisfy men. Each time I let the blade cut my flesh was to fix something I imagined would be unappealing to men. I'd mutilated my eyes, breasts, and vagina in a quest to find power as an object of desire. I thought if I was the most fuckable, I would be celebrated. Instead, my true self was erased, and I existed only for the consumption of men, a mere vessel for cum. My body was not entirely my own. I hoped to one day reclaim it.

LOLITAS

By 2008, my modeling and singing careers had stalled, derailed by shame and drug addiction, but I was swept back into a musical career after befriending hair metal–loving and bass-playing Katt Lee. I met Katt, a whirlwind of glitter and creativity, in her jewel-encrusted loft.

Despite my sputtering career, I still had a large social media following and took advantage of it to launch a jewelry line. Many friends had debuted streetwear brands like Diamond Supply Co. and True Love & False Idols, the latter of which my friend Alex Vaz then successfully sold his stake in. I trusted his recommendation when he referred me to Katt for my new jewelry project.

On meeting day, I pulled up to her massive loft on the second floor of a commercial building in the middle of the Diamond District in downtown Los Angeles (known as DTLA to locals). Confused by the closed Persian restaurants dotting the cul-de-sac and all the No Parking signs, I called Katt from my car.

"It's okay, I park there all the time," she chirped. "Coming down!"

Minutes later, she appeared at the side door with her Chihuahua in the crook of her arm.

"This is Toester!" she explained.

Alex would describe Katt as the Asian Patricia Field of our generation at her funeral years later. This was an apt description—at this first meeting, she wore a pink fur jacket over a T-shirt that read "Fuck Fashion" (using the Chanel logo for the "c"), a leopard miniskirt, and brown boots. Outside her already bursting closet were racks of bright clothing, furred, laced, and leathered. She was like an avant-garde unicorn-nymph with a heavy sheath of blunt-cut bangs, prancing out from a Gary Baseman painting. Many considered her a muse, and her apartment exploded with paintings and photographs of her likeness, dedicated to her by notable artists. She was like living art.

After that first meeting, we became inseparable, bound by shared passion for our new project, Hello Drama Jewelry. We had much in common, being the same age, and were the rare Asians enjoying hair metal when our generation of Asian Americans was mostly listening to hip-hop. Also, we both had pursued creative, nontraditional careers, much to the disappointment of parents who'd expected a more conventional path.

Although I occasionally contributed, Katt was the true creator. Her designs reflected our druggie emo vibes: shiny dangling Lucite crosses adorned with razor blades, glittery red syringes, and safety-pinned skulls. Eventually, the jewelry line inspired me to pursue music again, especially after learning Katt played bass. As a child, my mother forced piano on me, as well as a brief cello stint, hoping I'd join the junior orchestra. Despite resistance to mandatory classical music lessons, a connection to music seeped into my core as I toiled over theory and hours playing Chopin.

One night, as Skid Row's "I Remember You" blared from the iPod, an idea popped into my mind as we reviewed jewelry designs at Katt's place. "Would you ever play bass in a band again?" I asked Katt. I'd recently been inspired by Tila Tequila's Myspace success: her image had morphed from sexed-up import model into a sexed-up rocker with ripped T-shirts, black leather, and boots. She released original music and performed with a band. In 2007, she had about 1.7 million Myspace friends and debuted the song "I Love U," a guitar-heavy shouted rap-rock song produced by Lil Jon. Although the song didn't chart, it was the number one music download on iTunes.

"We should start a band," I said.

"YES!!" she squealed.

After discovering this synergy, things fell into place. Growing up, I'd idolized Guns N' Roses, Mötley Crüe, and Skid Row. Why was I trying to be Britney Spears? My childhood wasn't spent listening to pop stars like Debbie Gibson and Tiffany; I'd plastered my walls with posters of Axl Rose and Sebastian Bach.

We called ourselves Nylon Pink and posted calls for musician auditions on Craigslist and Myspace, assembling a lineup with a talented white male drummer and guitarist. With this new band, I saw an opportunity to escape the sexy Asian girl trope. Katt was a massive influence as an Otis College of Art and Design graduate and celebrity stylist. Her eclectic runway-driven style was not about displaying maximum swaths of skin; it mixed Japanese Harajuku street fashion and rock 'n' roll with a dash of Carrie Bradshaw and Betsey Johnson.

I wore skintight neon pants and a ripped-up shirt onstage like other rocker emo-scene kids. Katt might pair heeled leather boots with a glittery miniskirt and a clashing leopard print fur jacket. Our style inspiration was Myspace scene queen Audrey Kitching, with her hairspray-coiffed cotton candy–pink hair, raccoon-style eyeliner, and cacophonic mix of tutus, oversize sunglasses, and mixed patterns. My Chemical Romance and Panic! at the Disco were some of our favorite bands, and our goal was to play the Vans Warped Tour.

Kev Nish from Far East Movement produced our first song, "Hello Drama," an angry pop-punk confection that I cowrote. It had a hard-driving guitar riff and an angst-filled chorus we shouted/sang and dashes of girlish hope. My large but waning Myspace following, who weren't fans of my sexed-down reinvention, had a tepid reaction, and getting traction was a struggle. We mostly played local shows at dive clubs. But everything shifted in the band's second year when our white male guitarist left to finish law school.

We eventually found a replacement in Kiki Wong, a stunning Korean-Chinese guitarist we'd met during a photo shoot for Hello Drama Jewelry. We had cast her off the Model Mayhem website as one of the two models. She appeared at the door the morning of the shoot, quietly knocking.

"Is this where the shoot is?" she asked meekly, pretty even when bare-faced and shy. I was impressed by her flawless tan skin, high angular cheekbones, and sleek jawline. Over the next hour, the makeup artist transformed her into an almost mythical version of Asian beauty. Her eyes were extended and lined with long flourishes of sweeping eyeliner, and her silvery glittered lips matched the heavily chained aesthetic of our new jewelry line.

She strutted back on set, transformed from the young girl at the door. Now she towered over us in black stilettos. Her sleek black hair was crimped with a heavy froth of bangs framing her feline heart-shaped face. Dressed in a leather jacket and skintight black leggings embellished with a silvery reptile print, she was decorated with Hello Drama jewelry: a black spray-painted hair bow, stacked chain necklaces, and an anklet laced with silver crosses. On set, Kiki smoldered, changing poses in time with camera clicks, jewelry clinking with each pivot. Her metamorphosis and on-camera skills wowed me, and I pulled up her Model Mayhem profile during the shoot to study her portfolio.

"It says she was a metal guitarist!" I whispered to Katt, motioning toward the computer screen. I hadn't noticed it previously, but there was a paragraph detailing her musician past—mostly playing in high school bands—and her true passion: the guitar.

"I saw that you're a guitarist," I said to Kiki after the shoot. "We have a band!"

Her ears perked, and we scheduled her to meet our manager to assess her skills. She was expertly proficient, fingers gliding and tapping up and down the guitar neck. The timing seemed fortuitous; we had been unhappy with our then female guitarist's entitled and selfish behavior for some time now. The arrival of this even more talented and stunning player felt like kismet.

Months later, when our white male drummer left, we cycled

through a set of drummers, never finding a permanent fit. Eventually, our rhythm guitarist, Genn Ung, came across a flyer. It was for a show the following weekend in Orange County. A beautiful Asian female drummer named Jamie Scoles was performing.

Kiki drove down with Genn to watch her play and was dazzled by the tiny Vietnamese girl's skills, power, and stage presence. They waited patiently behind a line of fans after Jamie's set and invited her to audition for Nylon Pink. The following week, she did, although it was just a formality. We asked her to join immediately after she set down her drumsticks.

Our first gig with Jamie took place a few weeks later. As a teenager, Jamie was beyond excited. "Whoa! My first show with the band is on a rooftop?! This is incredible!" she exclaimed when arriving at the venue. The show was on the Standard Hotel's rooftop in DTLA. I've always hated downtown. It's a maze of one-way streets, and finding parking is a miracle. That night we were performing at a venue without a backline—aka a band setup—already on stage, so we had to lug all our equipment, amps, and instruments, including Jamie's entire drum set.

Nylon Pink was hired to perform at a Harajuku-style fashion show. We dressed Jamie in a black corset studded with tiny crosses and black leggings, a dramatic shift from her usual T-shirt and jeans. Kiki and I took charge of makeup, with our publicist Matt Rivera looking over our shoulders. As a natural beauty, Jamie didn't need any, but it was fun painting on her perfectly tiny, ideal Asian face with its angular cheekbones and perky pout. At five foot two, she looked like a miniature version of Kiki, who stood at five foot six. We couldn't help but notice how much they resembled each other. It was especially evident in the picture snapped before the set. The event photographer shot photos of us against the gleaming silver skyscraper–lined views of the city, the two guitarists' and bassist's instruments against their necks, ready to walk onto the stage. Jamie posed demurely in contrast to her taller twin, Kiki, who smized with all the minx energy of the fashion model she was.

As the lead singer, my job was to keep us in sync. Walking onstage, I turned to Jamie and reminded her to wait for my cue between sets.

"Make some noise," I shouted, as my bandmates cheered and clapped behind me. "We are excited to be part of such an amazing event. We're huge fans of Harajuku street fashion. Wasn't that an amazing fashion show? Make some noise for all the talented designers tonight." I paused for the applause. "Some of you might know this one. If so, sing along . . ."

Our manager wanted us to banter between all five songs, but I hated talking to the audience. I didn't have the natural flair for onstage small talk, so I wrote a series of scripts detailing everything we'd say the moment we got onstage through the end. I emailed it to my bandmates the night before for them to memorize. We played our standard twenty-minute set, featuring our original songs "Kiss Kiss Bang Bang," "Party Monster," and "Dirty in Pink."

Jamie played flawlessly, and afterward, as became the norm, several older men waited to compliment her performance. She was instantly a fan favorite. Though Nylon Pink had plenty of regular, non-Asiaphile fans, there was a very vocal contingent of older white men—many with Asian wives and girlfriends—who obsessively followed and supported everything we released. This was odd and unexpected, as the girlie, kawaii pop-rock music of the band certainly wasn't anything older men typically listen to. And they overwhelmingly favored Jamie over the rest of us.

The creepiest part was that though seventeen, Jamie could easily pass for a fourteen-year-old. She could even pass for a ten-year-old in some band photos. Jamie looked like a high school student. Two band members were stunning adult agency models, so the fact that Jamie was the most sexualized and popular was disturbing. She was the sole member with a dedicated following of old men lining up at her drum set afterward for a photo, autograph, or chat. She was constantly blocking middle-aged and even older men who stalked her and sent her disturbing messages on multiple social media channels.

Jamie also experienced a fair share of explicit comments from men in our orbit, including one rock promoter, who booked many of our shows and also those of iconic acts such as Muse, Katy Perry, Green Day, and the All-American Rejects. He was in his mid-fifties and had a well-known preference for Asian women. He became one of our biggest supporters and enthusiastically promoted Nylon Pink to his heavy-duty industry contacts, getting us more exposure, meetings, and shows. Working with men who loved Asian women was the path of least resistance. They were incredibly helpful, bent over backward to help, and were everywhere! These men seemed to enjoy simply being in the presence of young Asian women, and we were perfectly willing to accept their help. It was symbiotic, the helpful men orbiting around us, hoping for the sexual favors they never received, and us taking advantage of their base male desires. If we were going to be fetishized, why not milk it for all it was worth?

This promoter wore his edgy rocker persona like a banner, playfully enjoying our discomfort when spouting vulgar sexual comments. Jamie was a particular favorite to tease.

"Hey, little Jamie," he once called out as she laughed nervously. "You should meet me at my beach house later, and we could have some real fun. I'll show you my fun parts if you show me yours . . ."

We saw him as a trusted friend and mentor, so we dismissed the comments as his retired rocker style of banter, but Jamie—naive and sheltered—likely experienced some level of emotional damage from these comments, even if she wasn't aware of it then.

Our promoter also tried to convince us to start a side cover band called Miso Horny, a play on the derogatory phrase "Me so horny" from *Full Metal Jacket*. His brilliant concept was an all-Asian female rock band playing songs from the '80s and '90s on the Sunset Strip, like the comedic and super popular glam metal cover band Steel Panther. He thought Miso Horny shows should start with us scantily clad and eventually stripping down even more to just bikinis during our set. The band vehemently vetoed the idea.

I often felt it was my job to uphold our band's image and coach when necessary as the lead singer. My younger bandmates were like little sisters, and it was my big sisterly duty to help them grow. I encouraged Jamie and shy Kiki to flaunt their sexuality, often pushing them far past their comfort zones. From the start, I sexualized them, dressing them in skimpy, tiny pieces of clothing, forcing them to pose like pinups for photo shoots and smolder onstage. I considered myself the expert, as an entertainment industry elder. After all, I didn't invent the "sex sells" concept. Even as I pushed her beyond her limits, I felt protective of Jamie because of her age, but all I did was place her in the line of fire for Asiaphiles.

One instance I pushed Jamie too much was at a shoot with Neil Zlozower, who was our de facto band photographer. I met him years earlier after he messaged on Myspace to shoot, and we'd been friends ever since. With a heart of gold and a career spanning decades, he was in his mid-fifties and had photographed the most iconic album and magazine covers for bands such as Led Zeppelin, Van Halen, the Rolling Stones, Mötley Crüe, and Guns N' Roses.

We were recording a sound bite promo video for "Kiss Kiss Bang Bang," a song I wrote with the producer Clayton Ryan. Neil set up two silver walls of hundreds of mirrored squares. Each bandmate stood in front for a brief individual interview, commenting on the song cheekily. The song lyrics are thinly veiled innuendo about giving a blow job. In the makeup room prior to the shoot, while Katt outfitted Jamie in black jeans, a studded silver metal belt, and a ripped black crop T-shirt exposing an expanse of sleek abs, I tried to convince her to make cheeky comments hinting at the sexual nature of the song. It was too much for Jamie, who was so innocent.

"I can't talk about blow jobs on camera!" she protested vociferously in her makeup chair. She was so uncomfortable I eventually let it go.

When it came time to shoot, I marched confidently on set wearing a black bustier lined with circular silver metal trinkets and flirted with the camera as the song played lightly in the background. "I'll kiss the gun, just pull the trigger, and I'll play victim," my recorded voice sang, "shoot your weapon like a lush, I can't get enough."

"'Kiss Kiss Bang Bang' the song is about something that you have to interpret for yourself," I said. "Maybe you should really listen to the lyrics. It's about something that's explosive and very arousing."

Next up was KiKi. "'Kiss Kiss Bang Bang,' well . . . man . . . I guess there's a lot of ways you can interpret that," she said to the camera. "Um, mainly, I guess, it's up to you, or you can come to our shows and find out what it really means." She then broke character, morphing into her natural shy goofball state. "I don't know what the fuck I'm supposed to say. I don't want to talk about sexy stuff!!" she said, breaking out into loud and nervous laughter. "I don't know what to say," she screamed again in laughter.

Katt's answer was playful and ultra-girlie as usual. "'Kiss Kiss Bang Bang' is about flirting. You're kind of with a guy or girl," she said, laughing and twirling her body like an anime character come to life. "You're just kind of hanging out and things get heavy, and you know, it kind of leads up to an explosion of fun."

When it was Genn's turn, as the self-described butch lesbian of the band, she said matter-of-factly, "The song's about blow jobs, duh."

Finally, when it was Jamie's turn, for all my coaching efforts, she merely said, "We know how to play our instruments."

Looking back, I realize I pushed Jamie too much. Not everyone was comfortable capitalizing on our sexuality, and I failed to see the damage Jamie endured from endless Asiaphile interactions. At the time, I was doing what I thought was best after years of unsuccessfully chasing visibility without relying on this fetishized trope. When that didn't work, I dragged Jamie and my bandmates into using my tried-and-true brand of sexualized achievement.

Jamie's creepy older Asiaphile fanbase became even more trouble after we started covering K-pop songs. This was before Psy released "Gangnam Style" and BTS and Blackpink charted on the Top 40 lists (though the genre was already profiting from infantilizing and objectifying young women). Back then, K-pop was still niche, restricted predominantly to Asian American circles and hardcore fans. We first learned about K-pop from Jamie, a massive fan. The lyrics and melodies were catchy, and we covered K-pop songs in our hard rock format, featuring Kiki's heavy metal riffs.

The first song we covered was "Gee," by Girls' Generation, because of its more than 200 million views on YouTube. The song was an infectious earworm with an undeniably addictive melody. We translated the lyrics into English with an online translation tool, modifying them to run smoother but keeping true to the original lyrics, about a compliant young girl falling in love for the first time. She's timid, unable to breathe, and her body trembles at the sight of her crush. The message is she's so innocent and virginal that the sight of a man makes her nervous, an unconscious (or perhaps conscious) nod to the infantilizing and subordinating tropes of Asian fetish.

K-pop music videos further emphasize this infantilization of female K-pop idols as fragile, childlike, and innocent. They're a prime example of the concept of aegyo, characterized by behaving in a cute and childish manner, often expected in both male and female K-pop idols but more often observed in women. Through K-pop's dominance, this behavior has become mainstream in the West.

The "Gee" music video is filled with close-up shots of the individual members' exaggerated cuteness, winking, balling hands into fists and holding them by their cheeks, and poking index fingers into their cheeks while pouting. It is important to note that K-pop band members usually join the K-pop idol system as minors—as young as nine years old—and are subject to rigid and extreme patriarchal control. Idols are prohibited from dating to give the illusion of innocence and availability. The irony is that several retired idols have confessed they were forced to service much older music industry men sexually. They are often objectified pawns, commonly required to undergo extensive plastic surgery before their faces and bodies have even matured. There are strict beauty and weight requirements, and South Korea has the highest rate of plastic surgery in the world.*

After translating our version of "Gee," we laughed at the cheesiness of the original lyrics and the music video, but at the time, the inherent infantilization of women was lost on us. We went into the studio with our sound guy and producer to record our parts, adding our signature live instruments with heavy metal guitars. The song was released alongside an accompanying music video shot by Miles Flanagan at our rehearsal studio, which we shared with the Dreaming, a Hollywood band helmed by Christopher Hall, the former lead singer of Stabbing Westward, whose

---

* Although some argue that feminism means freedom of choice for women, it can't be ignored that one of the most patriarchally oppressive societies has one of the highest rates of plastic surgery in the world. It's been argued that South Korean women have been brainwashed into the belief that their only value is in their beauty, as judged by the male gaze.

popular song "Save Yourself" was featured on HBO's hit show *True Blood*. They were a bunch of tattooed white dudes, and both the lead singer and guitarist seemed to favor Asian women—one was married to an Asian woman, and the other had dated a string of them. The band was eager to share their rehearsal space, and the lead guitarist later became Kiki's boyfriend, allowing us to save quite a bit of money each month.

Most notably, we went full sex kitten with our wardrobe. In our previous photo shoot, we wore sexier clothing than we did in earlier shoots and received stronger reactions online, so we continued to push the envelope. Katt styled our new glamazon looks with Dead Lotus Couture, an edgy clothing brand specializing in skintight latex dresses that left little to the imagination, and accessorized us with piles of jewelry from our Hello Drama brand.

I needed to wipe Vaseline onto my thighs to pull my royal-purple dress over my body. The slinky little number accentuated all the right curves, with transparent cutouts exposing gratuitous swaths of skin, but I felt like a sausage, stuffed into casing. Mindy Holguin and three other makeup artists teased our hair heaven-high and shellacked our faces with thick layers of makeup from Mindy's own brand, Rag Doll Cosmetics.

Timid but model-beautiful lead guitarist Kiki, who got embarrassed whenever Katt and I discussed anything sexual, fit snugly into a rich chocolate-brown latex tank dress. The most significant transformation was pin-thin, natural beauty Jamie, clad in a teensy leopard print bustier, with jet-black clip-on bangs, fire engine–red lips, and layers of eyeshadow.

The video hit the internet on February 20, 2012, and countless

K-pop websites and blogs picked up news of our K-pop debut. "Girl Pop Rock Band 'Nylon Pink' Reveals English Cover of 'Gee,'" read the headline on allkpop, a top K-pop site. The reviews were mixed.

Although thousands loved our take on the K-pop classic, just as many hardcore stans hated us. They called us old and ugly, said we were sluts and ladyboys, accusing us of caking on too much makeup and wearing far too little clothing compared with traditionally "innocent and pure" K-pop stars.

Jamie, as expected, got a proliferation of swooning comments from her legion of old white male fans. All the online discourse and arguments drove up our views. After the success of our "Gee" cover, we continued to perpetuate Lolita stereotypes for likes, clicks, and views. In our band aesthetic, we doubled down on sexualized naivete, partnering with anime- and kawaii-influenced clothing brand J. Valentine. At our merch table, we sold a T-shirt with the slogan "Cute but Deadly" and described our sound as "Hello Kitty on acid."

We fully embraced the childish, cutesy Asian girl trope because it worked, but I've always questioned the underlying infantilization inherent in the Asian fetish. Asians often look decades younger than their ages, and there's the prominent intersection between youthful appearance and the idea that teenagers and children are easier to control and dominate.

The patriarchal infantilization of Asian women in East Asian media is exceedingly prevalent. We weren't the only female Asian group with an older male fanbase. The massive female Japanese idol group AKB48, with as many as eighty-eight members at a time, is famous for its younger members, some as young as twelve.

The oldest is usually a mere sixteen. They sing highly sexualized lyrics and appear in music videos and on magazine covers in lingerie despite being underage. The members have posed for the pornographic Japanese magazine *Weekly Playboy,* and several retired members have gone on to become porn stars.

Despite singing cutesy pop music, it's well known that the bulk of AKB48's fanbase is middle-aged men. This exploitation of teenage girls in Japan is a disturbing epidemic that inevitably spread to the United States through the proliferation of anime and manga. Although real child abuse images are banned, illustrated depictions are allowed in cartoons and artwork. There's an obsession with cuteness in East Asia. The well-known word *kawaii* translates into "cute," but it has more nuanced meanings in Japanese. According to Aris Teon, in his 2016 article in *The China Journal, kawaii* means "pitiable or poor," "something one should feel love for," and "something small or petty"; it "includes notions such as childish, benign, pleasant, but also desire, attraction and beauty."

The fact is, though pedophilic beauty standards for Asian women may have originated in East Asia, I've found real-life examples here in the United States. Most famously is the film director Woody Allen, an accused pedophile who married his ex-wife's adopted daughter, Soon Yi, who was ten years old when they first met. Another example is the actor Nicolas Cage—often accused of being an Asiaphile. There is no evidence he's a pedophile, but to me his current and fifth wife, Riko Shibata, could easily pass for fifteen years old or younger, especially as someone thirty years his junior. Similarly, his twenty years younger third wife, Alice Kim, also looked like a teenager when they married when he was forty.

Though his wives are of age, I still see an ick factor in how youthful they appear compared with him. The huge age gap creates an immediate power imbalance, with the much younger women at a disadvantage. Although dating much younger women is not unique to the Asian fetish, it's worth considering that Asian women appear more juvenile than their age and are already perceived as submissive. In this scenario, an Asiaphile dating a decades younger Asian woman seems suspect, as if he's searching for submissiveness, childishness, and servitude squared.

———

As our K-pop songs gained YouTube traction, Van Easterday, a Midwest music agent, reached out about booking our first tour. He teamed with our manager, Truck, to book a monthlong tour through Ohio, Missouri, Kentucky, and Illinois. Although Truck was great at booking gigs, he was a pure scumbag, a middle-aged white man with a childlike Asian girlfriend.*

His punk rock mannerisms included hocking loogies and constantly swiping at the bowl-cut bangs landing inches above his eyebrows. At first, he made creepy comments about Jamie's youthful looks until she dismissed his advances. She intuitively found

---

* I didn't keep in contact with Truck after I left the band. He's probably nearing sixty years old now. My friend forwarded an Instagram story he posted with his new girlfriend in the Philippines. I don't know her age, but she could pass for twelve, especially in the photo—she's smiling with a full set of metal braces, holding up a spoonful of whipped cream from her ice cream sundae.

Truck dishonest, disgusting, and unethical, and merely tolerated him with uncomfortable politeness. He took offense and started to harass her mercilessly, talking shit about her behind her back. He wasn't so different from the patriarchal K-pop system, expecting Asian women to be deferential and obedient no matter how crude and disrespectful he was.

Truck also treated us like pawns in his moneymaking machine. For our first tour, we had a tiny window of just over one month to learn and master dozens more songs to fit two seventy-five-minute sets (a whopping 2.5 hours of music). We were used to thirty-minute sets with five or six songs, but we now had to play forty songs to fill the required time for this tour. Truck knew but he didn't care how difficult the ask was. "Just fucking get it done," he barked unhelpfully.

We added rock covers of Katy Perry's "I Kissed a Girl," Adele's "Set Fire to the Rain," Lady Gaga's "Poker Face," and more. Jamie assisted immensely by adding four drum solos to the set. We threw together a CD for the tour for extra money off CD sales. It featured ten tracks, including our K-pop covers and original songs such as "My Religion" and "I Am the New Black."

The CD cover photo shoot with Phil Hernandez leaned into the innocent K-pop aesthetic. Jamie is wearing a giant pink hair bow and a furry white monster vest while jumping in the air, throwing two peace signs. Kiki is wearing the same hair bow while fluffing her cheeks with air and pouting in typical aegyo style. Our keyboard player Yuki Ito's white dress is festooned with massive lollipops and topped off with a dinosaur vest. She's balled her hands into fists and is posing with an aegyo-style baby face. Katt is wearing a furry skirt sprouting multiple tails, with one held suggestively next to her mouth. And I'm smiling wide—totally out of character—attempting to appear kawaii with huge purple hair, wearing a lime-green skirt with furry pink trim, nothing I would wear in real life if I wasn't leaning into this aesthetic.

After our preparations, we headed out in June 2012. Accompanying the five of us were our merch guy, our tour manager—a mini version of Truck named Chauncey—and our sound guy, who'd worked with us for six months. He was friendly and generous, but several of us found him slightly creepy. His favorite band member was unquestionably Jamie, whom he called "Scoles." To this day, I'm still not sure how good he was at running sound, but he was an Asiaphile who absolutely enjoyed touring around with this gang of young Asian women.

On tour, my relationship with Jamie began to unravel. By nature, I've always been jealous, and I found myself envious of the recognition Jamie received so effortlessly.

I'm the lead singer! I thought indignantly. *Shouldn't I be the most popular?*

Yes, she was hugely talented, and our younger fans certainly celebrated that. However, I doubt Jamie's older white male fans knew much about drumming.

When Jamie joined, she was like a little sister. I encouraged her to emerge from her shell—sometimes inappropriately—but also attempted to shield her whenever encroaching men crossed the line. Being in the band was like forming an instant family. We enveloped her, rallying around her like a gang of mother hens, always pushing her to the center.

However, a wedge developed during this tour as I stopped watching over her. Consumed by anxiety, I shifted my focus inward, determined to deliver my best performance. Once again, I found myself relying on the very sexuality I had tried to escape. It was taking a toll on my well-being, even as I dragged the women around me into the same trap. Like a mama-san, I forced the younger girls to shift sexuality to the forefront. But the worst part was how much attention Jamie received without trying. Despite my efforts to goad her into becoming a vixen, she never embraced it. We dressed her in skimpy outfits, but she remained awkward and uncomfortable. I hated that men adored her while I got scraps in comparison, despite actively seeking their validation.

Many performances were at bars filled with creepy old men. They were entranced when the gorgeous "sister" duo hit the stage, Kiki with her white Schecter guitar and tiny Jamie behind her drums. After shows, they'd accost Jamie or try to buy her a drink. Once a man of at least fifty grabbed Jamie's hand after she walked offstage. He dragged her toward the door and wouldn't let go until I pushed him off. After the tour, one of these old white dude fans sent Jamie extremely graphic, fetishistic, explicit, and racist sexual messages daily on Facebook and Instagram. She reported and blocked him, but he'd start new accounts to continue the harassment. At the time, I only noticed eyes on Jamie instead of me. I still based my self-worth on outside validation and felt competitive and defensive when it landed elsewhere. I was too self-absorbed to notice how uncomfortable the limelight made her feel.

On top of all the admiration Jamie was receiving, I felt she was turning into a princess. One night, after a disappointing bar show in the Midwest, we checked into our hotel room, a single two-queen bedroom for our entire crew of eight. Trying to conserve cash, we had booked the cheapest option. Jamie burst into tears after stepping in. She was a fastidiously clean germaphobe, and the room was filthy, with streaked shower walls and a grimy bathtub. The bedsheets were thin and stained, and a single roach skittered across the floor as we turned the light on. Since I'd already slept on the van floor for weeks, this didn't feel much different. I thought Jamie was being a baby.

"We are sleeping here tonight. It's already booked," I said, putting my backpack down and preparing for bed. Jamie ran outside crying, trailed by Kiki. Our merch guy, Tyler, followed the girls into the sketchy parking lot, and the three ended up sleeping fitfully in the van that night, Kiki with a taser in hand.

The stress of the tour transformed me into a hateable diva. We were utterly exhausted from the relentless schedule, having had no idea how overwhelming and taxing the whole experience would be. Jamie had it much worse than the rest of us. She had a four-piece Pearl drum set, and on more than one occasion, when there wasn't a backline, she had to load in, set up, and break down and pack up the set herself. It was an additional hour of work for her on those nights, even with our guys assisting her. Always diplomatic and fair, Jamie observed quietly as Katt and I would skip out on promotional activities, such as passing out flyers before or speaking to fans after the show.

"We already paid our dues! These younger girls just showed up to reap the benefits of the work Katt and I trudged, playing shitty shows in Hollywood," I shouted to Truck on the phone. "Make them do it! I'm exhausted. The lead singer carries the band onstage. Also, you all know I'm an introvert, and interacting with strangers gives me anxiety."

These became repeated excuses throughout the tour.

After each set, I ran backstage, leaving the younger girls to work the crowd. Unbeknownst to them, I was making my first attempt at sobriety and no longer had substances to quell my growing apprehension and discontent.

———

A couple of months after the tour, we shot a music video for our song "Heart Attack," a rock ballad with a memorable bell-like synth hook that Kiki wrote on a MIDI keyboard. The director and photographer, Ben Miller, emailed over the music video call sheet and treatment, writing, "The basic gist of the video is the girls arrive at a skate party to play a show. They all check out this hot guy. Then we cut back and forth between them interacting with him and them playing the song. Kaila wins him in the end, and the video ends with the conclusion of the big concert."

Although we had several potential leads for the music video, we cast our new vocal coach, Tony, a tall and brooding Italian with angular cheekbones and dark features. He had a sultry, melodious singing voice and was endearing because of his beloved Bengal cat, which he walked daily. Tony had given the band a group singing lesson a month earlier. I felt an unexpected nervous flutter as he entered my living room. During the lesson, we each sang individually for him to assess our levels, and I aimed to please and impress. I was too shy to converse besides asking perfunctory questions about singing. Jamie attended the lesson even though she didn't sing, and after class, she hit it off with Tony. They both skateboarded and had similar tastes in music.

I buzzed with excitement the morning of the music video. We were shooting at friend Dominic DeLuca's iconic skate shop on Melrose Avenue. Half Italian and half Greek, Dominic was a former heavy metal roadie for some of the biggest bands and a past host of MTV's *Headbangers Ball*.

We arrived as Tony was pulling up. I clammed up and ignored guys I liked, expecting them to take the lead, so I sped up, strutting ahead of him. Jamie bounded up to him naturally, chirping, "Morning!" and they bantered about what they ate for breakfast. I instantly felt annoyed and awkward, but I figured I'd have my moment with him later during the shoot. I focused on the exciting day ahead, as many friends would be appearing as background actors. My favorite part of being a musician has always been shooting music videos. This was my happy place.

Tony was the ideal male lead, and his charisma and talent shone through in the final edit. After the cameras were set, we started shooting each bandmate's scene seducing Tony. By midmorning, it was my turn, and there I was, face-to-face with Tony for our make-out scene.

"It's the luckiest day of your life. Act like it," our director said.

Tony looked genuinely puzzled. With his chiseled good looks, women threw themselves at him. It was hardly his lucky day to be fake making out with an older woman. I'd chosen my favorite pale denim dress from H&M with cleavage-enhancing bustier cups. The dress accentuated my hips and highlighted my legs—my favorite feature. We faced each other awkwardly in the storage room as the camera rolled with music playback. I vetoed any real kissing, so we started pretend making out, cheek to cheek, my hands rubbing his neck. I removed his shirt, and he ran his hands down my naked back as the crew watched. The cramped room was stifling, and with the camera inches from us, any urge to banter in between takes dissolved.

Afterward, we burst out of the back of the store for fresh air. Just outside, Jamie was fooling around on the store's skate ramp, expertly flipping her skateboard in her standard black skinny jeans and studded boots. "You know, you're not a terrible actor!" she told Tony as we emerged from the storage room.

"You know you're not a bad skateboarder," Tony replied, playfully pushing Jamie off her skateboard to showcase some of his moves. As they laughed and jostled, I stalked into the dressing room.

Shortly afterward, I saw Jamie at the craft services table. "You need to back off on Tony," I seethed, glaring. "I told you I was into him."

"I'm not even into him like that." Jamie looked genuinely puzzled. Her girlfriend was on set, and they were intertwined whenever we weren't filming.

"Just back off!" I snarled before walking off. I was frustrated at her easy, effortless connection with guys, so carefree and uncalculated. The most maddening part was she didn't even want the adulation and hardly noticed it. Dolled up with full hair and makeup and in a dress that was too sexy, I felt foolish. I had become a puffed-up and vainglorious diva and now more like a deflated balloon. Jamie barely lifted a finger, and men fawned. When I was her age, I needed to remove clothing for the same applause she received for merely batting an eyelash in jeans and a T-shirt. I didn't realize it, but I was resentful I'd spent such a massive effort baiting the male gaze, and she was so naturally charismatic that men flocked to her.

———

Years later, I discovered Jamie was more negatively affected than I had realized. She confided that her experience with Asiaphiles and creeps had long-lasting effects on her ability to form relationships with men. Although she had always been attracted to both men and women, she found it impossible to maintain relationships with men after Nylon Pink, having grown increasingly distrustful of their intentions. Her Asiaphile interactions left her with anger and resentment toward men, convinced they only cared about sex.

"Every guy I met while in the band sexualized everything," Jamie told me. "PTSD may not be the right way to put it, but it's a good way to describe the discomfort I feel around men."

Jamie never dated a man after Nylon Pink. Men swooned—everything I wanted—but she was left with disdain and disgust. Hers is a real-life example of the damaging effects of sexualized infantilization. Infantilization is inherent within Asian fetishism, with its themes of delicate, fragile, childlike Asian women dolled up as Japanese schoolgirls and anime Lolitas. We shouldn't brush aside these attractions and desires as harmless and complimentary. They can, at the very least, cause adverse psychological effects in Asian women and ultimately lead to violence against them.

For aren't such tiny, delicate objects easily breakable?

UNICORN

From the moment Katt and I met, we were inseparable. We reveled in our collective rebellious and kindred spirits. I had no idea our friendship and ventures would lead us deeper into a world that both validated and destroyed us. After Nylon Pink gained traction, Katt's fashion sense, once quirky, became more provocative. Alongside our publicist Matt Rivera's and my feedback, Katt, as our de facto stylist, dressed the band in increasingly sexier outfits, as her own style morphed. I was playing into the sexy Asian trope yet again, except now I had the power of five Asian women. As our popularity grew, I felt rattled. Our talent wasn't always the main focus as much as our looks and the fact we were Asian. Katt, however, seemed to find empowerment in the very objectification and revealing clothing I wanted to escape.

One of our first projects was recording the title track for the soundtrack of a movie starring Sonny Chiba and Danny Trejo. It was a Tarantino-esque action film where a woman seeks revenge after her husband is murdered in a heist gone wrong. The movie's theme centered around nyotaimori, translating roughly into "female body presentation." Known as body sushi, it's the Japanese practice of consuming sushi off a perfectly still, naked woman's body. It's a generally stigmatized practice in Japanese sex clubs. However, when co-opted in the West, it's often presented as some kind of highbrow Japanese cultural practice, a form of art. The sushi model and actress in the film is white.

We were on board after reading the synopsis from the movie producer. Our keyboardist, Genn, joined me in the studio to write the song with Mighty Mike, a multi-Grammy-nominated producer for artists like Carly Rae Jepsen, Dua Lipa, FKA Twigs, and Lana Del Rey. I cowrote the lyrics, and it's still one of my favorite songs. Called "One by One," it has an infectious chorus and could be described as a punky girl power anthem. The film producer approved the song and scheduled a music video shoot for the following week. We received an email with the call sheet, details, and script the Monday before the Thursday shoot. The script had us once again leaning into fetishized nudity, which none of us except Katt was willing to do.

My throat tightened as I read my directions. It began with me walking to the dining table in a "silken Asian black robe" and two chopsticks in my hair. At the table, I'd undress, the Asian robe cascading to my feet. Then it would cut to another shot of me lying on a table, completely exposed except for the bright green seaweed covering my breasts and pubic area. As I began singing, not moving a muscle, the band members would gently place pieces of sushi on me. There would be shots of all angles of my body, with the camera shooting from above and moving alongside me.

Each bandmate also had brief intercuts of herself naked on the table covered in sushi. During the heightened chorus, I would finally move, angrily shaking sushi from my body, leaving only three tiny pieces of glued-on seaweed. I would then crouch on all fours, seductively straddling a man.

I seethed, furious. My guess is the producer googled me, found naked photos, and figured I wouldn't have issues lying naked, only covered in tiny bits of sushi. He must have also believed his ideas worked especially well because we were Asian (though none of us were Japanese—falling into the false belief that all Asians look the same). I was willing to push a sexier band image, but I didn't want to be naked, even if it was just implied.

At band rehearsal, I pulled up the photos for the girls, saying, "Can you believe he wants us to wear this?"

"The photos he sent over are too naked, but if we just add some more flowers, we could cover it up more?" said Katt. "I don't mind shooting it." She had already started contacting designers to pull clothing looks for the music video and was excited. She had also started posting much sexier photos on social media since our popularity increased and seemed completely unbothered by the implied nudity the rest of us wanted no part of.

"No fucking way," said Kiki and Jamie as they shook their heads aggressively.

I shot off an email in reply to the producer. "Could we bring in another girl to play the sushi model? After speaking to each of the girls individually, they're skittish about the almost naked shots. They are super shy! We love the idea of bringing in the outside model or even using the movie actress or shots from the film. Also, we know many girls who could play the sushi model if you guys didn't have anyone specific in mind!"

The producer wrote back, explaining the individual skin-baring shots of each sushi-covered bandmate would only be three to four seconds max each and stressed there would be *no nudity* on camera. He called the sushi "appliances" and explained it would be like Adam and Eve and the Pussycat Dolls—tasteful. He explained that the "appliances" would be applied by himself and possibly a female makeup artist, adding there would always be a woman in the room during "appliance" applications, completely missing the point that we simply weren't comfortable exposing our bodies that way. And why did he assign himself the job of placing the sushi on our bodies instead of a female makeup artist or wardrobe person?

Our manager jumped in with an email. "During the first meeting over a month ago, it was not explained that the band would have to play sushi models. I would have put a stop to that immediately, as that is not a direction the band wants to be known for nor is it good for their brand."

The producer replied, refusing to use an outside model, claiming it was too confusing and that people would think she was a character in the film. He also refused to use the sushi model actress from the movie, insisting it would give too much of the movie away. He decided we should push the music video shoot to after the movie's post-production, regroup, and discuss it later.

We never heard from the producer again. About six months later, we discovered a cookie-cutter white guy band had replaced our band with an inferior song. They ended up doing precisely what we suggested: the sushi model movie actress played the sushi model in their music video. The men in the band certainly weren't required to lie naked on a table while the director placed sushi on their private parts.

———

Nylon Pink was swarmed by Asian-loving white men. The exploitation and objectification of women in the entertainment industry is rampant, so it's no surprise Asiaphiles flourished in this environment. Few paid attention before we became an all-Asian female band and amped up that imagery. It was as if having white guys in the band only distracted from the Asian fetish fantasy. I had started a rock band to break free from the sexy clichés I once embraced, hoping to carve out a new identity. But inevitably, almost unconsciously, I was drawn back in. While I felt unsettled by leaning back into old tropes and dragging other women into them with me, Katt seemed addicted to the newfound admiration, reveling in its power—as I did at the beginning of my modeling career. For her, the line between empowerment and objectification blurred as our hemlines got shorter. She had always been a muse, inspiring both artists and admirers, but the added layer of sexual allure seemed to embolden her. Scores of men were captivated by her with a fervor bordering on frenzy. She strung them along on a leash, flirting and playing into the trope of the ever-available Asian woman, but she was fixated on a renowned music producer named Tito with a known Asian fetish, and he kept her for years as his side piece. I despised him and judged their relationship so vociferously that Katt stopped confiding in me, causing a break in our friendship that only became more fractured once we started touring worldwide.

After our first monthlong tour in the Midwest, we booked our first international shows, including an Asia tour consisting of three weeks split between the Hard Rock Cafe Macau and the Hard Rock Hotel Penang. By now, we were a five-piece all-Asian girl band, like the United Colors of Benetton of Asians, featuring myself as the Taiwanese lead singer, Korean-Chinese lead guitarist Kiki Wong, Vietnamese drummer Jamie Scoles, and our two Koreans, bassist Katt Lee and the DJ Karen Beck.

We had a two-week residency at the Hard Rock Cafe Macau, playing three fifty-minute sets nightly. The set was stuffed with cover songs, as we didn't have enough original material for three hours of music. I expected the gig to be tough, but it was even harder than anticipated. Performing a one-hour set every night on tour is grueling, but three back-to-back sets with a ten-minute break in between gave me extreme anxiety. I did not have the training or endurance for it while battling jet lag and throat fatigue. Our sound guy, who later suffered from what appeared to be mental illness, didn't help. He had an unnecessarily complicated and time-consuming sound setup, making us sound worse, causing show delays, and pissing off promoters.

In addition to us band members, we traveled with our sound guy and tour manager. The Hard Rock put us in two three-bedroom apartments in two separate towers. After stressful nightly shows, we spent our days jet-lagged and sleeping, only venturing out to eat. My flatmates were Kiki and Jamie, and I gravitated closer to Kiki while distancing from Katt. Kiki and I loved to feast, and we'd wander the Macanese streets groggy-eyed to slurp new noodle dishes or gorge on delectably fatty roasted duck.

Life in Macao was Groundhog Day. After eating and sleeping all day, we shuttled to the Hard Rock Cafe. Dinners were included, and we'd arrive early to binge the Hard Rock menu: burgers, steaks, chicken tenders, chicken fajitas, mac and cheese, and milkshakes. We'd jump onstage, and in between sets, I hid in the dressing room, calling our manager back at home for support, whining about anxiety attacks. Katt and Kiki snuck back to chug alcohol—we had an open tab that they reveled in taking advantage of. After the relief of completing a set, we'd meander sweaty through the lobby, passing beckoning prostitutes in tawdry dresses and cheap stilettos.

While I wilted, Katt stole the show. She was effervescent with giggles, smiles, and flouncy hair tosses. Each night, she gifted a lucky male audience member a moment of attention, hopping on platform boots while cheekily plucking her bass guitar. I had difficulty connecting individually with audience members, but Katt pointed and drew them to the front of the stage by the sheer force of eye contact. One night, a handsome, tall, curly-haired blond guy watched, enraptured. We were all intrigued, but Tim only had eyes for Katt. Katt allowed him to buy her a cocktail, and they disappeared into the night. The couple was inseparable for the rest of our time in Macao.

On our last day, Katt brought Tim to dim sum. I liked him and hoped he could break Tito's spell. He was a sweet, wholesome finance guy from Texas working for an American corporation in Hong Kong and already adored Katt, as most men did. They dated for a year after we returned to the States. Although

Katt enjoyed her time with Tim, she wasn't in love, and the long-distance relationship eventually dissolved. Katt returned to Tito, who Katt said had gotten another Asian woman pregnant and bought her a house. He continued to string Katt along until she fell into a deeper decline, exacerbating her drinking tremendously. Like her nickname Kitt.E.Katt, Katt was like a feral cat—a healthy man could never tame her. Instead, she chased after toxic, unavailable Asiaphiles. Tim went on to marry another Asian woman. How would it all have turned out if he'd married Katt instead?

After Macao, we headed to our weeklong residency in tropical Penang, Malaysia. Although I boarded the plane in a terrible mood from our pathetic Macao performances, I was instantly bolstered by the warm tropical weather greeting us as we exited. The Hard Rock Hotel Penang had three pools of paradise spanning twenty-six thousand square feet. We each had our own hotel room for the duration of the stay, in sharp contrast to our Midwest tour, where the eight of us—the five band members and our merch guy, tour manager, and sound guy—sometimes slept together in one room.

In the stress of performing and the excitement of traveling, I had no idea Katt was beginning her downward spiral. Katt disappeared into herself more each day. She was still the bubbly, flirty presence on stage, but off stage, her drinking increased and she became secretive and vague when I inquired about her personal life.

Every morning, Psy's "Gangnam Style" blasted from the speakers; the song and the viral dance were inescapable that summer, the first in a series of crossovers over the next ten years, eventually leading to the mainstreaming of K-pop (I thought it was little more than a one-hit wonder fluke like "Macarena"). Between "Gangnam Style" and the success of our covers, K-pop, though in its infancy internationally, was beginning its reign over pop culture, but this tour was the beginning of the end for Nylon Pink.

Like in Macao, our rooms had an open food and bar tab, which many of us abused. We were a trite rock 'n' roll band stereotype, most of us with substance abuse issues. Six months earlier, I decided to try sobriety to fix the deep dissatisfaction continuing to permeate my life. It was unimaginably challenging to be freshly sober and touring with active alcoholics. An open tab plus twenty-four-hour room service meant a never-ending flow of fruity cocktails with pink straws and delicate pastel paper parasols. The poison from these fruity drinks flowed into the cracks and fissures within the band we didn't even know existed—we were each secretly combating internal demons. While I struggled to endure my daily sobriety battle, the rest of my band was lulled into an alcoholic, summer-soaked, piña colada–infused haze.

Katt retreated, and we weren't even aware of the rip currents drifting us apart. We had always been a solid tag team. Katt was the nurturing, gentle, motherly influence, whereas I was the hard-driving, domineering, typically spoiled, and entitled lead singer. Katt usually supported my decisions, but in Malaysia, she turtled into her obsessively secretive, alcoholism-fueled world. She leaned deeper into her sensuality, posing in suggestive bikini and lingerie shots as she became perilously skinny.

I was, in turn, preoccupied with my personal sobriety journey and found myself annoyed by her inability or lack of desire to sober up. Her struggles were more profound than I realized. I had just recently started examining my past and started therapy. My healing work forced me to take a hard look at my motives and the unconscious desires that had shaped the trajectory of my life. With the guidance of therapy and a twelve-step program, I waded through the muck of my past, sinking into a deep depression as I confronted buried traumas, decisions, and intentions. As Facebook and Twitter eclipsed Myspace in popularity, I also mourned the fading of my former notoriety. My complicated feelings about my pinup model years roared back with a vengeance. After a decade of pursuing music, I questioned if it had been a complete waste of my life.

As a teenager, I dreamed of men worshipping me, and it came true for a moment. The attention satiated my ego, but it never filled the God-size hole inside.

"No man will ever want to date you," my mother had screamed after finding my *Playboy* photos. Her comments struck a nerve I stuffed down—that it rang true. I thought I was proud of my beautiful images. "I'm an empowered woman," I would exclaim to naysayers. But my mother's words reverberated. *What kind of respectable guy would want to date you?*

My whole life's motivation was seeking male validation, first as a pinup and now as a sexy lead singer. I had actively attempted to escape my natural sex kitten inclination, but mainstream media didn't allow my success outside of this restrictive box. It was easier to submit instead of constantly fighting the patriarchy.

My biggest revelation on tour was this: I didn't actually enjoy performing live. I loved dolling up and shooting music videos, but I was more enamored of the idea of being a singer and addicted to the self-worth I gleaned from it. It was the camarade-rie, the feeling of being part of a crew of striking and talented bandmates, that grounded me more than the spotlight. Still, it was the same dynamic I'd orchestrated since high school, finding affirmation with a bevy of stunning women while playing into toxic masculinity–manufactured Asian fetish tropes. It felt like a double-edged sword for Asian women in the music business. We were celebrated for embodying a fetishized fantasy, but our true selves remained invisible; we were mere constructs and cari-catures. The renown wasn't validation, it was a trap, and we were selling ourselves short.

Our Asia performances were not a wild success. Our various addictions overtook our individual lives. Without drugs to numb my inhibitions in early sobriety, I had crippling performance anx-iety. More than once, I forgot the lyrics to one of our dozens of new cover songs, turning my back to the audience and pretending to interact with Jamie, hoping no one would notice. Our manager expected we'd wow the Hard Rock executives in attendance, in-spiring them to book us on a Hard Rock world tour, but they snuck out without saying goodbye. We arrived home defeated and humbled. The band went on hiatus, needing a break from the chaos and disappointments of recent tours and to cocoon our-selves in the holiday season.

After about a year of sobriety, I quit the band but stayed on to help with management. Over the following year, we auditioned several new singers and eventually sent the band on another Midwest tour with a fresh lead vocalist. The tour was so tumultuous that both Jamie and that lead singer quit the band before the tour's end, forcing Kiki to take over lead vocals. Soon afterward, the Misfits scouted Kiki for their new female rock band project, She Demons, and she left Nylon Pink for the bigger opportunity. Nylon Pink officially ended in 2015, and all bandmates eventually pivoted to different projects. Over the next several years, I became a published writer, Jamie became an operations director at a wellness company while playing drums on the side, and Kiki continued touring as a guitarist, eventually joining the Smashing Pumpkins; but Katt never found her footing again. Kiki also got sober, and we hoped Katt would find her way there also. But despite getting a DUI and being forced to attend AA meetings, Katt vowed never to give up drinking.

"It's just death and drama—oh well, let's just drink" was one of Katt's catchphrases. Alcohol was her balm, and she loved saying, "Live hard, die pretty."

After Nylon Pink disbanded, I rarely spoke to Katt directly, although we were all on a Nylon Pink group text. She chimed in every few days, often musing nostalgically about the band, but the rest of us had moved far beyond ever wanting to reunite. Katt became highly reclusive and always had an excuse for skipping out when the rest of us gathered for Korean barbecue. Then the pandemic hit, and we were forced to quarantine and shelter in place, only keeping in touch via group chat. Although Katt popped in occasionally on the chat, we were accustomed to her disappearing for weeks.

On November 17, 2021, Kiki and I met up for one of our regular lunches.

"Have you talked to Katt?" she asked me.

"I haven't spoken to her in forever . . . but Katt's gonna be Katt. I feel like one day we could just find out she passed," I blurted out.

We looked at each other nervously and laughed it off as a silly thing to say.

As if a prophecy, the next day, Kiki got a call from T. J. McDonnell, our former drummer and Katt's ex-boyfriend.

"He said her parents have been blowing up his phone and that no one can reach Katt," Kiki said. "T.J. asked if I was still in K-Town and could go check on her, but I didn't know how to get into the building. Her parents are freaking out and are driving down from the Bay Area today."

"I'm sure she'll turn up," I said. It wasn't rare for Katt to vanish and reappear out of the blue, acting as if nothing had happened.

The following morning, my phone rang at 8:00 a.m. I knew what Kiki would say the instant I saw her number appear at this early hour.

"She's dead," Kiki said, her voice deep, throaty, and flatly monotone. I can't remember that day's sequence; it was a flurry of phone calls, shock, and condolences. The worst part was thinking of her parents, who hardly spoke English, and the fact that they'd lost their only child.

Over the next week, as friends pieced together what had happened, we discovered none of Katt's close friends had seen her in person in at least two years. T.J. was one of the last to see her, and he said she had fallen into a severe depression since turning forty. It was as if she'd systematically cut out every significant person in her life so no one could observe her decline. Katt died of liver cir-rhosis and didn't tell a single close friend about her diagnosis, al-though she'd known for at least a year. It's a disease more common in men and people over fifty years old and is most commonly linked to heavy alcohol consumption.

Besides the heartbreak of losing a sister, Kiki and I were shaken by the realization that if we hadn't gotten sober, we could've easily met the same fate. If I hadn't examined my past under a glaring microscope, I might still be chasing the power I briefly possessed—propped up by the fleeting glow of male admiration, fading along with my youth. It felt like after we disbanded, Katt couldn't reconcile the loss of her identity as a sexualized Asian bombshell. I could relate: that attention is fiendishly addictive.

Asian fetish tropes reduce Asian women to flimsy caricatures, but there is no denying the validation it satisfies for certain dam-aged women. Although the Asian fetish is degrading, feeling de-sirable when you're vacant of self-worth is acutely compelling. Asiaphiles frequently gaslight Asian women into considering themselves lucky, rationalizing fetishization as a compliment. As I wrote in my *Newsweek* op-ed, they convinced me to believe: "What young woman doesn't want to be part of a group so desir-able that there is a well-known term to encapsulate that obses-sion?"

The fetish dehumanizes us—and makes it much easier to enact violence. That gaslighting causes us to question our reality, mentally draining us so we overlook the dehumanization of hypersexualization and grasp for the imagined power bestowed on the anointed. Sometimes we lean into fetishization, not realizing its inherent foundational spiritual and emotional damage. When it ends, we're like hollowed piñatas, paper-thin and more emotionally empty than ever. Without the fool's gold of male validation, we're nothing but a gaping void.

In some cases, the harm is deadly.

Katt, I feel guilty for dragging you into this temporarily fulfilling yet dangerously addictive world—one that reels in young women with promises of empowerment, only to release them, sending them plummeting, when they're used up, leaving them feeling hollow and desolate but desperate for another hit.

It could have been me.

A RECKONING

Remember their names:

Daoyou Feng

Xiaojie Tan

Soon Chung Park

Delaina Ashley Yaun Gonzalez

Paul Andre Michels

Hyun Jung Grant

Suncha Kim

Yong Ae Yue

On March 16, 2021, a lone white gunman strolled purpose-fully into Young's Asian Massage near Atlanta, Georgia. After re-ceiving services, he fired his 9mm handgun at everyone in sight and left. He followed up with a shooting spree at two other spas, killing eight people in total, six of whom were women of Asian descent.

After the news flashed onto my cell phone screen, I refreshed *The New York Times* website all night for updates, pasting headlines into my group chat with my former bandmates. The girls were equally shocked. We commiserated about the same disquieting pit at the bottom of our stomachs. I felt a deep well of helplessness and reexperienced my past trauma.

We were still living amid a vicious news cycle of Asian hate, watching elderly grandmothers get smashed into sidewalks and murdered in broad daylight. I also found myself reliving my earlier compliance with yellow fever tropes, feeling distasteful and guilty as I was confronted with the most extreme example of violence that can come from fetishization and hate. Asian Americans were collectively exhausted from the recent slog of AAPI hate crimes and shocked by this new one, but not surprised. We saw it coming.

It was the confluence of the Asian fetish, the model minority myth, our purported adjacency to whiteness, and a pandemic with Asians of all ethnicities blamed and targeted by attacks both verbal and physical. We saw it coming when we tried assimilating but were still packaged as other, alien, and exotic. We saw it coming when hordes of people on the streets started yelling, "Go back to your country," to us, our friends, and our family. We saw it coming with your Asian fetish.

After hearing mostly Asian women were killed in the massage parlor, my friends and I instantly knew Asian fetish was the motivation. The shooter's later defense was sex addiction and a desire to eradicate the women at the spa, whom he saw as "temptation." The media and police department denied the shooting was motivated by fetishism and Asian hate, stating he was simply having a "bad day." But he was a frequent visitor at Asian spas and clearly viewed Asian women as objects he had privilege to use, dominate, subjugate, and then eliminate when he was finished. No matter how much we assimilate or achieve, we're still objectified, invisible, silenced, and gaslit.

The shooting wasn't an isolated incident of fetishism-fueled violence against Asian women. In 2016, a German man murdered his Filipino wife, Grace Koenig, to go on a Thai sex holiday and sleep with prostitutes. In 2018, a white American tourist in Japan decapitated his Japanese Tinder date, Saki Kondo. His mother later said it was his dream to marry a Japanese woman. In 2017, two men raped, tortured, and burned a twenty-eight-year-old Vietnamese woman named Quyen Ngoc Nguyen. Prior to the murder, one of the men texted the other, "Are we raping the chink?" In 2018, the NorCal Rapist, a fifty-eight-year-old married man who worked at the University of California, Berkeley, and targeted and raped ten Asian women over the span of twenty years, was arrested. In an article for *The Cut* titled "What White Men Say in Our Absence," Elaine Hsieh Chou summarizes the gruesome online post "List of WMAF [White Male Asian Female] Violent Crimes that Made the International News," writing, "Women dismembered and melted in sixty liters of acid, women stabbed 76 times in the chest, women sliced up and boiled in a pot, women choked and tortured to death, women sawed into eight pieces and stored in a locker, women molested and photographed in disturbing positions after they'd been killed. One hundred and three pornographic DVDs were found at one murderer's home; 51 featured Asian women."

Most troubling is that many of these murderers were men who were romantically partnered with Asian women, not strangers.

There are way too many others to list. Most incidents received scant media coverage. As throughout history, Asian voices were silenced, erased, and dismissed. If we hadn't been amid a global pandemic originating in China and experiencing a sudden surge in Asian hate crimes, would these spa shootings also have been forgotten?

Many of these acts mirror what appears in Asian-themed pornography, which continues to be extremely popular and often violent. In their paper "Gender, Race, and Aggression in Mainstream Pornography," Eran Shor and Golshan Golriz found that "aggression was present in three-quarters of the videos containing Asian women, a much higher rate than for any other group of women in our study," and that the Asian women "performers" were of the China doll variety, "passive, submissive, or eager to please."

In the study "'Click Here': A Content Analysis of Internet Rape Sites," by Jennifer Lynn Gossett and Sarah Byrne, the researchers studied pornography featuring rape or forced sex. They found an "overrepresentation of Asian women on Web sites selling rape." Their work cites other studies linking violent pornography and assaults against Asian women. Sia Nowrojee and Jael Silliman, in their contribution to the 1997 collection *Dragon Ladies: Asian American Feminists Breathe Fire*, make a connection between pornography and crimes, like the rape of a twelve-year-old Asian girl by U.S. servicemen at the Okinawa military base. The scholar Helen Zia, in her essay "Where Race and Gender

Meet: Racism, Hate Crimes, and Pornography," connected the 1985 rape and murder of an eight-year-old Chinese orphan girl named Jean Har-Kar Fewel to a *Penthouse* pictorial of Asian women in bondage and torture poses published two months earlier. In 2014, two Indonesian women, Sumarti Ningsih and Seneng Mujiasih, were raped and tortured to death over the course of three days in Hong Kong. The culprit was a rich white British banker who watched violent pornography and recorded his victims for pleasure.

The Atlanta massage parlor shooter also spent hours watching online pornography, suffered from sex addiction, purchased massage parlor sexual services, and went on a shooting rampage against the porn industry. In an interview with *The Washington Post*, the culprit's former roommate said, "He hated the pornography industry. He was pretty passionate about what a bad influence it was on him. He felt exploited by it, taken advantage of by it." We have no idea if the shooter watched violent or Asian porn, but the link between pornography and his violence was directly stated.

Men with yellow fever often claim that Asian women are preferable to white women, whom they view as overly demanding and masculine, with the assumption that Asian women are on the opposite side of the spectrum—easier to control. These stereotypes are certainly perpetuated in porn, and it's not surprising that these ideas can eventually lead to violence. Porn is often the truest representation of societal beliefs at a given moment.

Over the next few weeks, the memories of my modeling and singing careers erupted like a dormant volcano, shooting regrets to the surface, melting the seal I had carefully wrapped them in and submerged deep inside myself. It had been ten years since I'd left it all behind. I thought fondly of that time but had moved on.

I had since morphed into a travel writer and grew a significant TikTok following speaking about Asian American culture during the pandemic. I occasionally posted videos about my modeling days, but that era of my life was no longer in the forefront. But when news about the shooting broke, I was reminded of my questionable choices and the media influences of my youth. It forced me to reflect on how much the Asian fetish was the driving force of my teens and twenties.

Most Asian women hate the Asian fetish. I spoke out derisively about it in public, yet in private chats with Asian girlfriends, I might say, "Well, obviously Asian girls are the best, there aren't any fetishes about any other ethnicities of women, are there?" Accordingly, I used the Asian fetish to my advantage and secretly enjoyed it when it benefited me. I co-opted it for profit and personal gain, even while growing up in a middle-class family with two parents providing for all my needs.

This was in sharp contrast to fifty-one-year-old single mother Hyun Jung Grant, one of the eight victims of the shootings, whose financial situation forced her to take treacherous and poorly paid jobs to support her family. "She died working for us," said her twenty-three-year-old son, Randy Park, in an interview about his mother for *The New York Times*. "It's just unfair. She already didn't have much of a life to begin with." He and his twenty-two-year-old brother, Eric, live alone now. Grant was forced to work a fetishy job to support her family, and a white man killed her because of it. She didn't have my privilege to slip the Asian fetish "coat" on and off. She died because of yellow fever, and I was completely unscathed—physically at least.

Stories like Grant's demonstrate the costs and real-life repercussions of the seemingly harmless yellow fever trope. The Atlanta shooting forced me to stare into the face of that intersection of misogyny, racism, and poverty for Asian women. Mainstream media considers Asian Americans to be the model minority. I've fallen into believing in this narrative at many points in my life. My parents believe in this manufactured story, as do countless Asian Americans. In the minds of many, we have achieved the American dream as "honorary whites," ignoring the massive swath of Asian Americans living in poverty. Systemic violence disproportionately affects them, and few realize that almost one in four Asian New Yorkers suffered in poverty in 2020.

But the model minority myth and the Asian fetish act as erasure, presenting the illusion that Asians have achieved the pinnacle of the American dream with Asian women as the most desirable. Internalized racism teaches Asian women they can escape racism through assimilation and their proximity to whiteness. It's a modern-day version of Manifest Destiny, the narrative of white saviorism, the colonialist and entitled belief that it's the white man's supposed duty to "rescue" the Asian woman from her supposed plight. This is evident in the proliferation of white supremacists dating Asian women for their perceived docility. Many Asian women fall into their trap, subconsciously trying to escape racism (see Audrea Lim's 2018 article "The Alt-Right's Asian Fetish" in *The New York Times*). For much of my life I chased this very mirage of escape from discrimination. In fact, I realized I exploited the Asian fetish for my gain once again, just two weeks prior to the spa shootings, on a walking date with a possible Asiaphile.

I absolutely hate walking dates. It's impossible to make proper eye contact, and if a guy won't even spring for coffee on the first date, that's a red flag. As a writer, I'm comfortable meeting strangers and making them feel at ease. However, these skills disappear once I start ambling along. Being naturally clumsy, the juggling act of trying to look cute, keep my balance, and deliver witty banter simultaneously is a disaster waiting to strike. After the pandemic, I joined Hinge out of boredom and a bombardment of walking date invitations rolled in. Sure, they made sense during the pandemic, but I was in no rush to meet anyone. I hated them so much I opted to wait until we all got vaccinated and could meet normally again.

That is, until I matched with my celebrity crush.

Well . . . celebrity is a stretch, but he cowrote one of my favorite movies growing up with his famous writing partner. Many regard this writer as a comedic genius, but he's far from conventionally handsome. I discovered him on Netflix even though I don't watch stand-up. My ex-boyfriend loved comedy specials, and I'd annoy him by half watching along while scrolling through Instagram the entire time. But when he turned on this comedian's special, I put my phone down five minutes in—and was instantly hooked. This comedian joked unflinchingly about his battle with depression and introversion. I appreciated his fearlessness and vulnerability, and he mentioned he was in a twelve-step program (like me!). My ears perked up when he said his girlfriend was

Asian, and the icing was when he cracked another joke about his Asian woman favoritism.

Usually, it's a turnoff when a guy has an Asian fetish or has dated a string of Asian women. It's not necessarily a dealbreaker, but it's certainly a red flag. But I dismissed the signs, telling myself that since I had an instant crush on this self-described damaged man, he got a pass. Instead of seeing it as my usual negative, here I considered it a major plus, assuming this Asian preference (possibly fetish?) worked in my favor. I'm not usually a fangirl, but I decided that this somewhat obscure comedian was my one celebrity crush.

Years after watching his comedy special, we matched on Hinge as I was shopping at Target, mindlessly swiping while wheeling my cart through the home goods aisle. I was shocked when his face popped up on my screen. I couldn't believe it. Was he a catfish? I tapped the "match" button, and he messaged me ten minutes later. I almost tripped down the stairs walking back to my car.

"Hi," he wrote. I felt a surge of breathless excitement and wanted to screenshot the message to show as proof to my friends but didn't want to jinx it.

"You're a comedian?" I asked, referencing his profile description and pretending I hadn't already watched hours of his comedy specials and his movie at least ten times growing up. I quickly unfollowed him on Instagram and Twitter to keep up my ruse. In a state of blissful, purposeful ignorance, I brushed aside warning signs, like his possible Asian fetish and his debilitating depression and refusal to treat it with antidepressants. I suffer from depression, have taken Prozac for years, and know firsthand how miserable untreated depression is. Remaining hopeful, I thought, *Wouldn't I understand him better than anyone else?*

But then came the dreaded question: "Do you want to go for a walk?"

No! I thought but agreed anyway. It was Tuesday, and when he suggested Thursday, I countered with Sunday, so I didn't seem too available. But as the days crawled by, I wished I'd agreed to Thursday, as the nervous buildup was unbearable. By Sunday, I hadn't heard from him and finally caved and texted him a few hours before the date to see if it was still happening.

"Meet me at 5 pm in front of McDonald's," he replied. There was a McDonald's within a walkable distance from my house, but it was unsafe to walk around in the area after dark. Also, I wanted to wear knee-high boots with heels that weren't made for walking instead of tennis shoes, so I drove. In the short drive to the meeting spot, Paramore's "Still into You"—a high-energy, uplifting pop-rock song—blared through my car speakers as motivation.

"Just parked," I texted, checking my makeup in the mirror. I'm never nervous for first dates, but I was anxious for this one. Pandemic mask etiquette added another layer of stress—do I approach with it on or off? I decided to slip on my standard blue surgical mask as I stepped out of the car. As I approached, he had on the most distractingly large and yellow face mask, making him look like a mash-up of Hannibal Lecter and a human wasp.

"Hi!" I exclaimed, probably too loudly. Seeming uncomfortable with direct eye contact, he threw his body into motion. I scrambled to follow, tripping slightly behind him and hoping he didn't notice.

"You're a loser!" an unhoused man reeking of urine trolled, pointing at the comedian as we rushed past him.

"You know, two people died in a gunfight around here just a week ago," I said, trying to spark a conversation. He seemed irked by the man's commentary, and I wanted to defuse the tension. The sun was beginning to set, and I hoped he'd suggest dinner. "I think walking dates are silly, but I made an exception for you," I added.

He didn't respond directly to anything I said. Instead, sliding his mask off, he said, "I just got a vasectomy," a strange revelation five minutes into our date. I thought, *That's great. I'm child-free. Bonus points for me?*

"I don't want kids myself," I said. "I mean, people who have kids just want to make carbon copies of themselves, amirite?" I joked, trying to get a laugh, slipping my mask off to match him.

Without addressing my comment or laughing, and slipping his mask back on, he said, "My famous comedian friend said to me, 'You just got a vasectomy so that you can fuck as many women as possible!'"

I galloped behind him to match his walking sprint—were we in a race? When I caught up, I had missed the opportunity to ask, "Well, was *that* the reason you got the vasectomy?" I slipped my mask back on to mirror him.

"Have you ever been married?" he asked abruptly, catching me off guard.

Well, there's no small talk with this guy, I thought, before answering, "I've never cared about it, but I'm not opposed. How about you?"

"I'm open to it," he replied, sounding unenthused.

After just four blocks, he said, "Let's cross here." As he slipped his mask off again, we crossed the street and headed back toward our cars. By now, I was thoroughly confused about why he kept randomly slipping his mask on and off without explanation. On our brief walk back, he bragged about his upcoming projects and name-dropped many celebrities. I'm uncertain if he cared if I was listening, as I trailed behind him the entire time. Suddenly we were at his car.

"Here's my Tesla," he said. "I'll text you."

He jumped in his car and drove away without so much as a "good night" or "goodbye." I stood in shock for a minute, thinking, *He's not even going to walk me to my car? It's dark, and we've established that the area is unsafe.*

After speed walking to the safety of my car, I sat staring into space, unable to comprehend how the date went so horribly wrong. Even so, I hoped to hear from him. Over the next week, I replayed the date over and over in my head. Did I say something stupid? Was it because my jokes fell flat, or did he only want anti-marriage women? I doubted myself and my actions but never paused to question why I was so fixated on this man who was kind of a dick and had untreated mental health issues.

A week after the date, the shooting occurred. Because of it, I started writing more stories about Asian American issues and highlighting Asian voices in my writing. My articles were published in magazines like *Rolling Stone* and *Business Insider* and on websites like *Mic*, and I wondered if the comedian would come across my work and think of me. Call me delusional or insane, but I thought he might message me after the shooting, as many of my non-Asian friends and acquaintances did, checking if I was okay. After all, he publicly spoke out as an ally to disadvantaged communities.

When he didn't, it finally hit me. Because of his comedic genius and fame and how that sheen might rub off on me, I admired this man who had treated me dismissively. I later learned he'd publicly made derogatory comments about Asian men. Coupled with the jokes he made about his Asian women preference, there were red flags all around, but I ignored them because of my fangirling. Just because I admired his comedic brilliance didn't mean his flaws—or possible racism—got a free pass. It was purposeful ignorance—a habit I indulged far too often in my youth. I'd turn a blind eye to red flags, allowing myself to chase desires without restraint. His flippant behavior was indicative of standard Asiaphile practices, treating us as unworthy of basic decency. Like the spa shooter gunning down his victims because of his rage over his own fetish, some men with yellow fever don't think we're human.

I'm still hardwired to replay this old behavior, abusing the Asian fetish when it's to my advantage and when it suits me. I'm still in the process of uncovering the unconscious ways I perpetuate this cycle. It's something I'll need to remain vigilant about and continue unraveling, likely for the rest of my life. But the shooting surfaced this programming into my consciousness. My bubble burst. I realized I had to aggressively challenge this narrative that had been driving my life for decades, as the irreparable harm it caused was now blatantly obvious.

It's painful to realize that I may have contributed to violence against Asian women because of the selfish ego-stroking I gleaned from fetishization. At the time, I didn't know how deeply these ideas permeated my thinking. The shooting jostled a reevaluation of my life's choices, and I was shocked by my discoveries. I felt guilty and culpable, yet sorry for that young woman who turned entirely to male validation to heal the gaping hole of self-hate. I don't regret the past. I believe you learn from mistakes and that sometimes the worst experiences are the most instrumental building blocks for character growth. But I know if I had different influences growing up, my choices would have been different. Popular media plays a crucial role in advancing efforts to portray Asian women beyond sex objects.

"The problem is invisibility, so the solution is visibility. . . . We need to be seen in our full humanity," explained the activist Amanda Nguyen during a panel on anti-Asian violence hosted by Axios.

Growing up, the only visible Asian women in pop culture sold sex. From the Fook Mi and Fook Yu twins in *Austin Powers in Goldmember* to the Vietnamese students having an affair with their adult gym teacher in *Mean Girls* to Sung-Hi's glossy calendars and magazine covers, sexualized Asian women were everywhere.

Luckily for young women today, pop culture is responding and changing exponentially. I'm still shocked to hear Korean words sung on LA's most popular radio station, KIIS-FM, as K-pop dominates headlines and airwaves. Since the shooting tragedy, countless Asian American–centered projects have debuted or been greenlit. Back in 2018, *Crazy Rich Asians* was a watershed moment. We were so grateful for the most visible nonstereotypical Asian representation in decades, but since then, our growth in media has been sky-high. There has been such a wildly successful proliferation of Asian-forward projects that I can't list them all, including Netflix's *Squid Game* and *Beef, Everything Everywhere*

All at Once, Shang-Chi and the Legend of the Ten Rings, and *Joy Ride.* I'm so excited to see Jennie, Rosé, and Lisa from Blackpink successfully launching their solo music careers in the United States—all girls known on a first-name basis. I wish I had this kind of representation growing up, and I'm incredibly grateful that young women today have stronger role models, because I certainly wasn't the best.

During my modeling days, young women often reached out, sharing their dream to become an import model like me. Some Asian Americans have told me my role in *The Fast and the Furious: Tokyo Drift* is iconic. I appreciate the compliment deeply, but it's sobering considering I said only two words in the entire movie and was on-screen for no more than ten seconds. I was mere eye candy in booty shorts. My cameo was not groundbreaking, and it showed how sparse media representations were; we were desperate to celebrate *anything.* We grasped at crumbs of representation, even the most objectifying and trivializing exposure.

No woman should ever feel as restricted as I did, believing that reducing myself to fit a male fantasy was the only way to be acknowledged. This isn't to say that women shouldn't feel empowered in their sexuality. Women should embrace their sensuality as much as they like, as long as they have full agency and are free from external pressures or control. For me, leaning into that aspect of myself wasn't genuine, and I was acting from a place of low self-esteem. In contrast, healthy sexuality—rooted in personal agency and authenticity—should be celebrated.

I hope young women today will make better choices and that, by sharing my imperfect, damaged, and yet hopeful story, more young Asian women recognize their multifaceted beauty, focusing on inner strength over physical appearance. I dream of a day when young women stop releasing so much power to men, realizing their vast and limitless set of qualities are far more enduring and valuable than sexual desirability.

We cannot ignore the implicit misogyny behind the Asian fetish and how it's portrayed in the media. It's imperative that we continue to fight to be heard and be seen in the media as multifaceted beings.

Representation matters.

DEEP

Through therapy and the development of a spiritual practice, I've spent years processing the trauma of my assault, as well as the layers of unexamined self-objectification and internalized racism. Daily meditation has been essential for reconnecting to my body in ways I had forgotten. Inner child work has helped me re-parent that lost and unwanted little girl who felt she had to fend for herself. Cultivated self-love has become a vital skill, replacing the fleeting gratification of male attention. One of the greatest gifts of tuning into my inner desires has been discovering my passion for water and animals.

After reading *Deep*, by James Nestor, I developed a zeal for freediving and its healing and restorative effects. At first, I wanted to compete. Freediving is one of the few sports in the world where you can start middle-aged and become a champion. My idol and one of the greatest freedivers in the world, Natalia Molchanova, started the sport at forty and won twenty-three gold medals before her tragic and untimely death. It's considered one of the most dangerous sports in the world, but I was drawn to the serene silence of underwater submersion, my love for marine life, and the profound connection I felt with my body each time I submerged beneath the waves. I signed up for champion freediver Lance Lee Davis's freediving and spearfishing class, excited to take my first steps in this new sport.

Freediving often appears glamorous on Instagram. In one video, I'm plunging into the transparent azure waters of Bora Bora, a seven-foot manta ray gliding gracefully beneath me. My feed is filled with svelte, lithe young women with perfectly sculpted derrieres in tiny bikinis, their long fins slicing the water as they swim alongside dolphins and other sea creatures. But freediving in California isn't pretty. I can't bring my carefully styled blowout, lip gloss, and winged eyeliner underwater.

My Performance Freediving International (PFI) freediving class took place in early December, and the water in Redondo Beach was about fifty-five degrees. I purchased an unflattering camouflage 5mm hooded wetsuit for the occasion, topping it off with gloves and booties for warmth.

Getting past the wave breaks was intense. I entered the frigid salt water with a five-pound weight belt strapped around my waist and long fins under one arm. At first, I attempted to jump through the wave break, which knocked me underwater, almost causing me to lose my mask. I soon learned it's much easier to dive straight in and under the waves, swimming furiously and blindly in the murk to emerge past the break. From there, it's a seemingly endless fifteen-minute swim to the diving spot.

I was exhausted after arriving at the buoy and line our instructor had dropped to measure our diving depth. My dreams of competition were quickly dashed. Although our first training session was in a twelve-foot-deep pool, it couldn't prepare us for the feeling of diving underwater headfirst into the open ocean. To pass level one, we needed to consistently hit a depth of sixty-six feet, about the length of a six-story building. At just thirty feet, I was quickly stumped with equalization issues, unable to do the tricky Frenzel—a complicated technique using the epiglottis to push air into the nasal cavity—to relieve the pressure in my ears and sinuses.

Disappointed and frustrated, I returned home and devoted weeks to learning everything I could about equalizing. I watched videos, took classes, and read whatever I could find, but I still couldn't master this technique.

I was heartbroken until I realized that, once again, I was pushing my body for results instead of simply enjoying the practice of freediving. I was so accustomed to using my body like an object and tool, devoid of compassion or feeling for it, instead of appreciating my incredible vessel. It wasn't so different from using my body in pinup modeling to gain validation, power, and attention from men, twisting my body into uncomfortable contortions for photos and going under the knife for further desirability. I spent years playing the part of the China doll, the dragon lady, and the hypersexualized Asian schoolgirl that fetishists desired. Growing up shy, it was the only way I managed to feel sexy, desired, and in control of my body. The result was violent objectification, both by men and by myself. The brutality of my youthful fetishization choices shaped the trajectory of my life and relationships with men, resulting in trauma, depression, dissociation, substance abuse, and twisted relationships.

Objectification is the act of stripping away one's identity, reducing one's body and sexuality to parts and tools to be used. By warping my body into unnatural poses and playing the role of the lustful Asian woman, I engineered myself into a robot—none of that mechanical performance was authentically me. The aftermath left me attempting to piece together the broken doll parts of myself and reclaim what I'd lost. Yet here I was, repeating the same ingrained habits, pushing my body beyond its limits, ignoring my own humanity, and transforming myself into machinery to compete.

After this realization, I set aside my champion freediver ambitions and embraced the simple joy of drifting in the ocean and the meditative experience of entering another world. Freediving is one of the most personal and intimate ways to connect with the ocean, and this can be achieved at any depth. It reminds me of the natural magnificence of my body and its many intricate processes that are beyond my understanding. It wasn't created for superficial lust or leering, gawking eyes. The sport has helped me connect to the healing balm of the ocean, washing away shame so I can be bodily present and alive. Underwater, I feel the lingering dissociative trauma stored in my solar plexus soften. I reclaim my body, no longer plucking at and prodding it like an instrument, and revel in its pure being.

As a teenager, I became Kaila Yu to shield my true self, Elaine Yang. Elaine was a weak and pitiful victim, but Kaila was strong, fearless, and unbreakable. Creating that alter ego was necessary for self-preservation. It was a form of self-distancing, a coping mechanism allowing me to step outside of myself to control my emotions, reduce anxiety, and increase confidence.

However, as much as my alter ego was protective, the layer of armor grew so thick it shielded me from authentic connections. It made me tough, hard, and brittle, filling me with masculine energy—leading with the results. Now the focus is on letting my feminine energy guide me—leading with feeling and embracing vulnerability. There's no longer a need for a protective outer shell to fend off online attacks, ridicule, and public shaming. Instead of being driven by shallow, ego-based exteriors, I want to cultivate deep bonds of friendships and meaningful relationships. Free-diving has helped me connect to my body authentically, freeing it from object-based behaviors. It's washed away layers of pro-grammed misconceptions about self-worth and its former intrin-sic connections to youth and external beauty. Getting sober was also integral. I was no longer a feral cat, lashing out in terror to protect herself.

The best part is that I feel more beautiful in my forties than ever. Although I wish I'd enjoyed the breezy beauty of my youth, I was too mired in and dependent on the whims of outside validation and judgment to take pleasure in it. Today, I love myself and am finally confident in my skin, and I'm so grateful my looks have no impact on my current career. I know the best in my life is still to come.

I wish my younger self knew I'd brought Kaila Yu and Elaine Yang closer together. I'm hoping someday they fuse into one.

SOURCES AND ADDITIONAL READING

Over the course of writing this book, I read several books and articles about yellow fever, feminism, and the history of racism against Asian American women. I owe a debt of gratitude to the historians, journalists, and scholars who wrote about this topic before me and am including a short list of the books and articles I consulted for those who want to dig deeper into the history of Asian fetish.

BOOKS

The Asian Mystique: Dragon Ladies, Geisha Girls, and Our Fantasies of the Exotic Orient by Sheridan Prasso

Dealing in Desire: Asian Ascendancy, Western Decline, and the Hidden Currencies by Global Sex Work by Kimberly Kay Hoang

Dragon Ladies: Asian American Feminists Breathe Fire edited by Sonia Shah

Embracing Defeat: Japan in the Wake of World War II by John W. Dower

Geisha, a Life by Mineko Iwasaki

The Hypersexuality of Race: Performing Asian/American Women on Screen and Scene by Celine Parreñas Shimizu

Marginal Sights: Staging the Chinese in America by James S. Moy

Reshaping the Female Body: The Dilemma of Cosmetic Surgery by Kathy Davis

Rise: A Pop History of Asian America from the Nineties to Now by Jeff Yang, Phil Yu, and Philip Wang

Unbound Voices: A Documentary History of Chinese Women in San Francisco by Judy Yung

ARTICLES/ESSAYS

"The Alt-Right's Asian Fetish," Audrea Lim, *The New York Times,* January 6, 2018

"The Asian Baby Girl (ABG) Through a Filipina American Lens," Stacey Anne Baterina Salinas and Talitha Angelica (Angel) Acaylar Trazo, *Alon Journal for Filipinx American and Diasporic Studies,* 2023

"'Click Here': A Content Analysis of Internet Rape Sites," Jennifer Lynn Gossett and Sarah Byrne, *Gender and Society* 16, no. 5 (2002)

"Dating While Asian at Penn," Angela Huang and Arina McGinn, *34th Street,* February 18, 2018

"Gender, Race, and Aggression in Mainstream Pornography," Eran Shor and Golshan Golriz, *Archives of Sexual Behavior* 48, no. 3 (2019)

"Mainstream Porn Has Taught You a Lot About Asian Female Sexuality—But It's All a Result of Racism," Amy Sun, *Everyday Feminism,* April 13, 2015

"Orientalism and the Binary of Fact and Fiction in *Memoirs of a Geisha,*" Kimiko Akita, *Global Media Journal* 5, no. 9 (2006)

"The Start of American Accommodation of the Chinese: Afong Moy's Experience From 1834 to 1850," Tao Zhang, *Journal of American Studies,* October 31, 2014

"Uncovering History of Double Eyelid Surgery," Claire Lee,
   The Korea Herald, September 11, 2015

"What White Men Say in Our Absence," Elaine Hsieh Chou,
   The Cut, March 24, 2022

"Where Race and Gender Meet: Racism, Hate Crimes, and
   Pornography," Helen Zia, 1995

"White Sexual Imperialism: A Theory of Asian Feminist
   Jurisprudence," Sunny Woan, *Washington and Lee Journal of Civil
   Rights and Social Justice Law,* 13 (2008)

A NOT ENTIRELY COMPREHENSIVE LIST OF FETISHIZED PORTRAYALS OF ASIAN WOMEN IN MAINSTREAM MEDIA

The Toll of the Sea (1922)

The Thief of Bagdad (1924)

A Girl in Every Port (1928)

Shanghai Express (1932)

China Girl (1942)

Japanese War Bride (1952)

House of Bamboo (1955)

Love Is a Many-Splendored Thing (1955)

The Teahouse of the August Moon (1956)

Sayonara (1957)

The Barbarian and the Geisha (1958)

China Doll (1958)

South Pacific (1958)

The World of Suzie Wong (1960)

A Girl Named Tamiko (1962)

Tamahine (1963)

You Only Live Twice (1967)

Madama Butterfly (1975)

Shōgun (1980)

An Officer and a Gentleman (1982)

Year of the Dragon (1985)

Tai-Pan (1986)

Full Metal Jacket (1987)

Come See the Paradise (1990)

Indochine (1992)

Madame Butterfly (1995)

Chinese Box (1997)

Charlie's Angels (2000)

Rush Hour 2 (2001)

Austin Powers in Goldmember (2002)

The Quiet American (2002)

Kill Bill: Vol. 1 (2003)

The Last Samurai (2003)

Lost in Translation (2003)

The Sleeping Dictionary (2003)

2 Fast 2 Furious (2003)

Harold & Kumar Go to White Castle (2004)

Mean Girls (2004)

D.E.B.S. (2004)

Memoirs of a Geisha (2005)

Sin City (2005)

The Fast and the Furious: Tokyo Drift (2006)

Silk (2007)

Gran Torino (2008)

Machete (2010)

Scott Pilgrim vs. the World (2010)

The Social Network (2010)

The Wolverine (2013)

Ex Machina (2014)

Miss Saigon: 25th Anniversary (2016)

ACKNOWLEDGMENTS

Thank you to my editor, Amy Li, for championing my book and for her brilliant feedback. I couldn't have written this book without her. Thank you to my agent, Amy Bishop-Wycisk, for believing in the book when it was just an idea. Thank you to everyone at Crown, especially Kimberly Lew and Lauren Chung in marketing and publicity, as well as Joyce Wong in production. I feel so lucky to have you all on my team. Thank you also, to the team at The Future Of Agency.

Thank you to the best mom ever, who taught me strength and unconditional love. Thank you to my dad, one of the solid and trustworthy men I know, and thank you to my brother, Eric, for standing by me despite my difficult years. Thank you to my bandmates and musical family Kiki Wong, Jamie Scoles, and Matthew Rivera for permitting me to share a bit of their stories.

Thank you to Mike Dunphy for teaching me how to write. Thank you to my precious action group family Tim Courtney (my action partner bestie), Kelly Sullivan Walden, and Lucinda Faraldo. Thanks to Shannon Collerary for her priceless feedback and multiple readings and directions. Thank you to Annie Jacobsen for your invaluable mentorship.

For those who saved me through the tough times while writing this book and spent hours on the phone with me and on text, thank you to Mccready Baker, Peter Cohen (my breakup bestie), Arleen Milian, Sarah Jones, Helena Diep, Scott Goldman, Dominic Deluca, and Neil Zlozower. Thank you to all my amazing followers on TikTok and Instagram. Thank you for giving me the platform and voice to write this book.

Thank you, Katt Lee, for your sparkle. It inspired me in ways I'll never forget.

About the Author

—

KAILA YU is a freelance writer for the *Los Angeles Times*, *Rolling Stone*, *The New York Times*, *Business Insider*, *Condé Nast Traveler*, and more. Formerly, she was a model and the lead singer for the all–Asian American female rock band Nylon Pink.